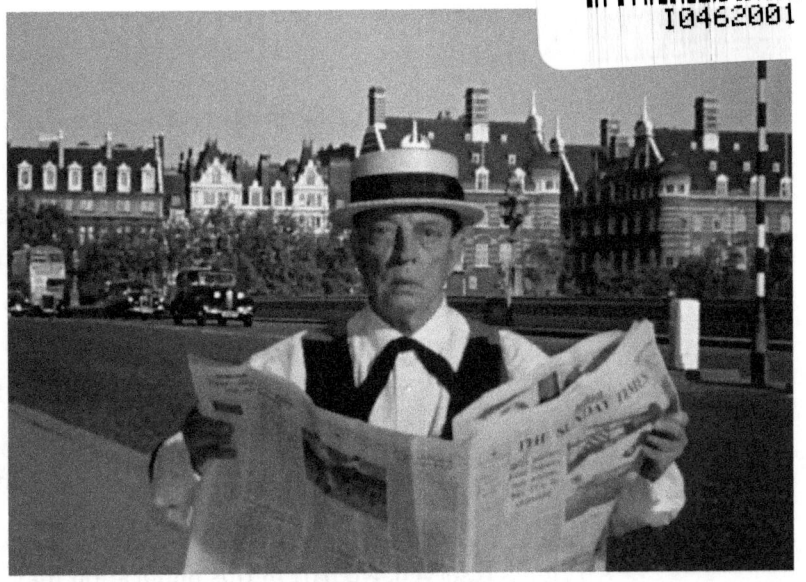

BUSTER KEATON

THE LATER YEARS

By Chris Wade

BUSTER KEATON: THE LATER YEARS

by Chris Wade

Wisdom Twins Books, 2018

wisdomtwinsbooks.weebly.com

This edition released in 2018

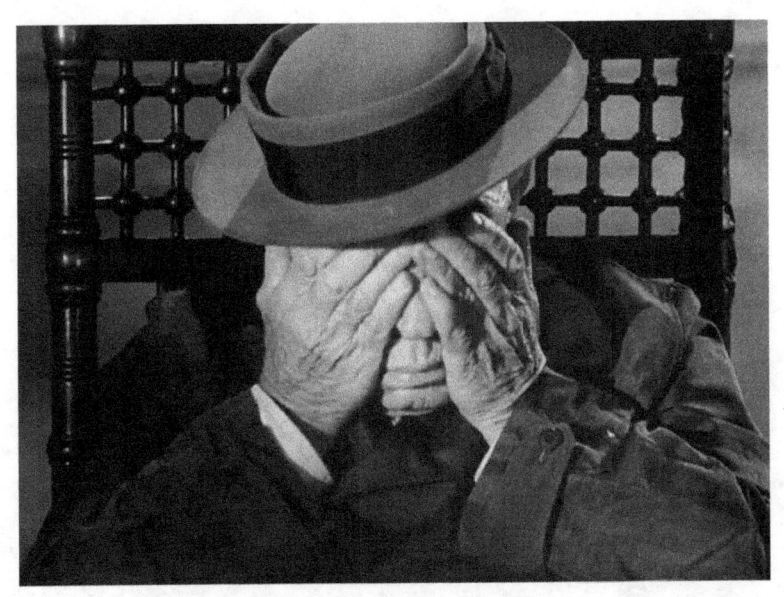

BUSTER KEATON

THE LATER YEARS

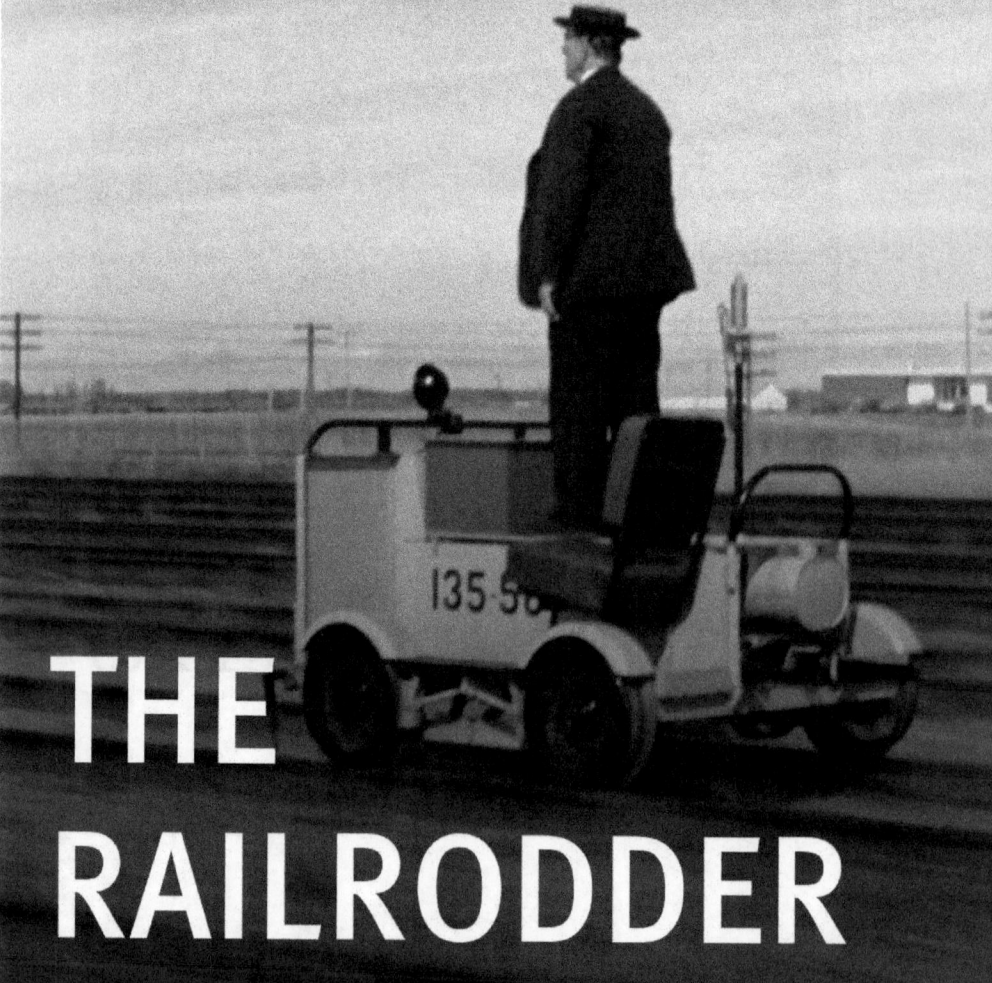

THE
RAILRODDER

"Off camera Buster was a busy, sociable guy who laughed and talked his head off. Never a dull moment. He seemed to really love people and despite some really bad personal years he loved life and certainly loved his wife Eleanor who shared his sociable personality."

- Gerald Potterton (director of The Railrodder) to the author

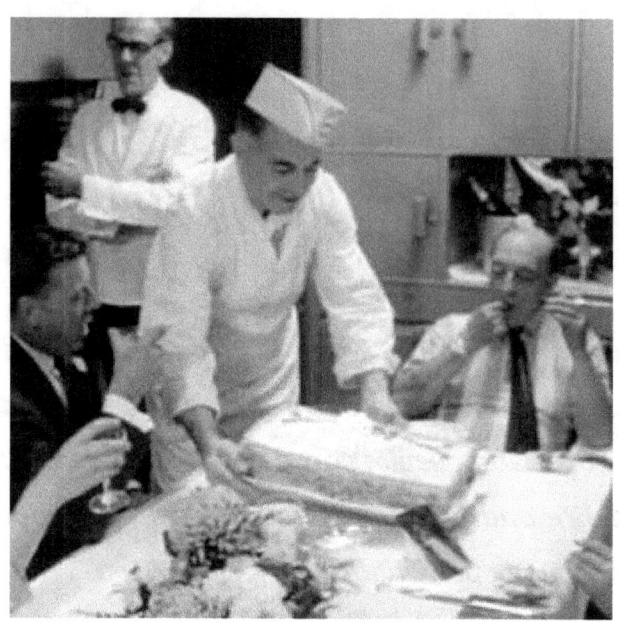

CONTENTS

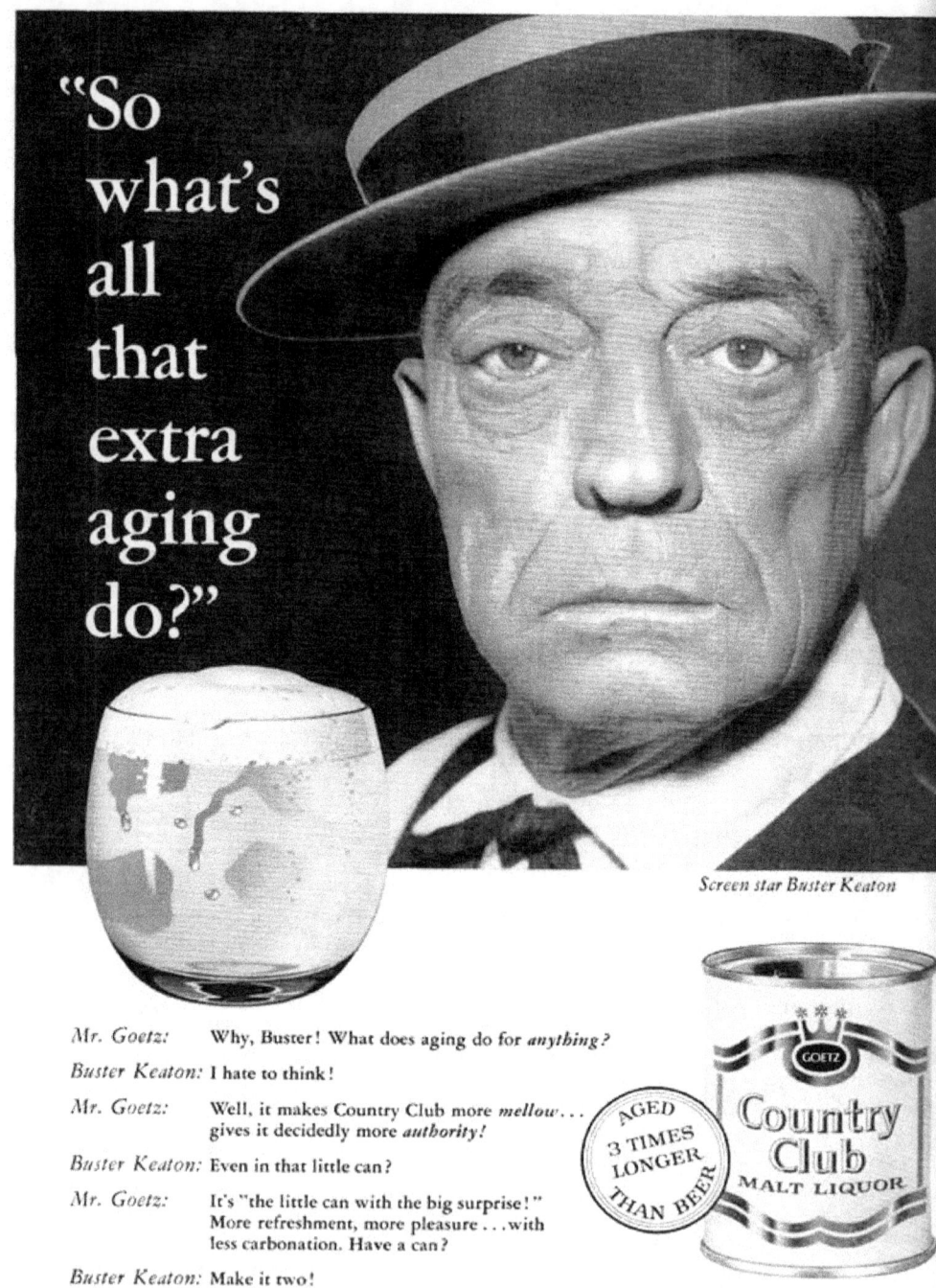

"So what's all that extra aging do?"

Screen star Buster Keaton

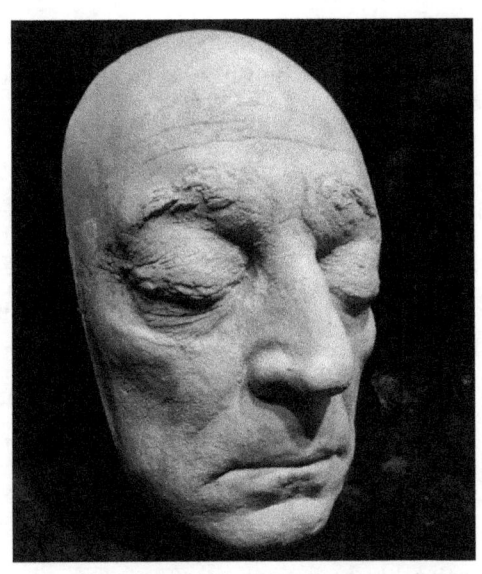

<u>INTRODUCTION</u>

A Misplaced Genius

There's a wonderful scene in the marvellous 1965 documentary, Buster Keaton Rides Again (all about the making of Buster's classic short film The Railrodder, and his quest across Canada during its shooting), where Buster is presented with a cake by the crew on his 69th birthday. As they enter the room singing the birthday song, Keaton stares down, his eyes averting away from the adoring crowd in embarrassment. Rather sweetly, he nervously chews his finger, and for that one moment, looks like the shyest man on earth. For some reason, despite the countless classic scenes and moments he has given us in his cinematic masterpieces, this is always the image that pops up in my mind whenever I think of Buster Keaton.

Most people would think of one of the breathtaking stunts, maybe the one in Steamboat Bill Jr. when he stands still as the house comes tumbling upon him, his small body saved by the open window frame without which he would surely have perished. Maybe the image of him hanging off the front of the train in his 1926 masterwork The General. Perhaps the washing line sequence in Neighbors, or the scene in Sherlock Jr. where, as the projectionist, he walks out of his own sleeping body and into the motion picture showing at the cinema. There are so many unforgettable moments in Buster's filmography - I could reel a hundred favourite moments off if I wanted to - but for some strange reason, I always think of the elderly Buster, humble and shy as the birthday cake comes towards him. He has the classic, relatable mannerisms of a man uncomfortable with being the centre of attention (not knowing where to put his eyes, too embarrassed to even smile), which makes the fact he is one of silent film's most famous and adored stars all the more ironic. This is the key to understanding Buster as a man and artist, the sad looking clown who made some of the greatest films in history, but couldn't handle a crowd, the legend without ego.

Keaton is an icon, no question, and he belongs firmly in a special area of film legend - the silent clowns. Buster is up there with Charlie Chaplin, Harold Lloyd and Laurel and Hardy in this special reserved hall of fame. But simply lumping him in with anyone else, even such adored figures as the aforementioned names, is doing Keaton an injustice. He was a genius in his own right and very much in his own field, an independent auteur who, given free reign by the studios, paved the way for others. He was a man who took the flack for the sake of future generations of directors, everyone from Woody Allen to Orson Welles, anyone desiring creative freedom in fact. He made some of the finest films of his era and was one of the most famous film stars on the planet. He went against all odds and made movies which, even by today's standards, are visually stunning feats.

Though Buster's posthumous reputation is immovable, and steadily growing, Keaton's career timeline while he was alive and working does not entirely match his rich legacy. Despite making profitable films that also won rave reviews from the critics, Keaton battled with studios for his artistic freedom - and eventually lost it. But he was a tough one, a grafter who focused on whatever job was at hand, however degrading or weird it may be; a working entertainer, just happy to be still stand, and of course working, even when times were leaner than they once had been.

Buster's career was sprawling and winding. He began as a side man for famed movie clown Roscoe Arbuckle, became a solo star in his own right with a series of classic shorts, then established himself, with Chaplin, as a leading actor-director in the twenties. But it wasn't all plain sailing. Unbelievably, The General did not fare well with audiences or critics upon its release in 1926, and Keaton lost final cut on his future work. Contracts became hugely limiting, and Keaton no longer owned himself. Signing with MGM, he became a product, and one that the Hollywood system had considerably less interest in as the silent age ended and the talkies came in. This revered genius was now a has-been, a faded face from the past in only a matter of years.

Worse still, Keaton became a drinker, lost his mansion, as well as his wife and his children, in a very messy divorce. In his forties, he was working as a gag writer on the films of other comedy stars, like The Marx Brothers, and it took some time before his achievements were properly recognised and Keaton himself was accepted as the true innovator he was. In fact, though he experienced a latter day renaissance, Keaton didn't earn his deserved reputation until he was dead.

These days, Keaton is one of the most important figures in the history of movies, and has influenced all manner of filmmakers and comedians from all walks of life; Monty Python, Richard Lewis, Jackie Chan, Woody Allen, Mel Brooks, Wes Anderson, Bill Murray... the list goes on. Besides his innovative comedic skills, Keaton was also a maker of true masterpieces, awe-inspiring work which in my opinion is still unmatched to this day. Even Orson Welles once claimed The General was the Greatest Film Ever Made, the very man who directed Citizen Kane, a film frequently finding itself in that position.

What always fascinated me most though, as great as Keaton's golden period remains, were his latter days, where his fortunes turned around, and he slowly built his way back from annihilation. People tend to divide Buster's career on film into two categories, pre-1930 and post-1930, before and after the arrival of sound. They speak of a decline of which he never recovered. Of course, I disagree with this theory totally, and value some of his later works as much as I do the classics. In his sixties, while most comics were in the show business retirement villages, reclining and looking at their scrapbooks, Buster grafted on, working on TV, on stage, and in films, delivering performances that were just as consistently daring and impressive, perhaps more so, due to his old age and the ravages of time. His chaotic, excellently conceived silent shorts were mainstream entertainment in the 20s, and millions came out to see

12

them. But by the 1960s, though the originals were classics just being rediscovered by avid viewers whose parents weren't even born when they were made, any new experiment in that field was considered surreal and avant-garde; films like the afore mentioned Railrodder, and Samuel Beckett's Film, also released in 1965 and starring Keaton in one of his most odd ball roles. Keaton always had an expressive face (those bug eyes, the sadness behind them at all times) but as an older man he seemed even more characterful, those features coming vividly to life as the years went on, despite rarely even having to move or change them.

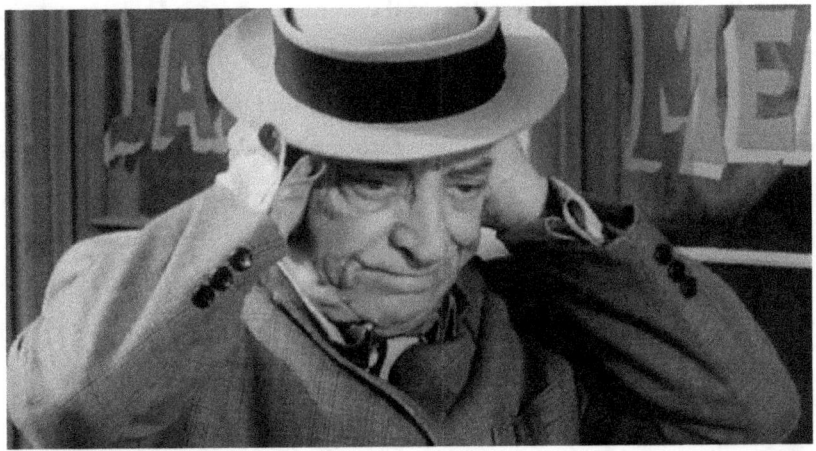

The elderly Keaton looked almost like a caricature of the younger one, with those huge bulging eyes and solemn glances. In truth, he often looked weighed down by something; which is odd, for in his final years he was anything but glum. Indeed, he had very little to be sad about. Friends, family and colleagues recall a happy, sociable man who loved to work and tell tales of the silent era. It conjures up some lovely images for sure, and shoots down the negative rumours of a washed up, bitter old clown.

Keaton's reputation saw a dramatic turn around in the later part of the 20th century, but he wasn't around to see it. People like Roger Ebert were calling him the master of his time, and writing rave retrospectives on films like The General. "Buster Keaton was not the Great Stone Face so much as a man who kept his composure in the centre of chaos." Ebert wrote in the late 90s. "Other silent actors might mug to get a point across, but Keaton remained observant and collected. That's one reason his best movies have aged better than those of his rival, Charlie Chaplin. He seems like a modern visitor to the world of the silent clowns."

In the same piece, Ebert charts the decline and gradual rise again of Buster and his work: "In less than a decade, from 1920 to 1928, he created a body of work that stands beside Chaplin's (some would say above it), and he did it with fewer resources because he was never as popular or well-funded as the Little Tramp. Then the talkies came in, he made an ill-advised deal with MGM that ended his artistic independence, and the rest of his life was a long second act--so long that in the 1940s he was reduced to doing a live half-hour TV show in Los Angeles. But it was also long enough that his genius was rediscovered, and he made a crucial late work, Samuel Beckett's Film (1965), and was hailed with a retrospective at Venice shortly before his death in 1966."

Ebert makes Buster's later years sound rather sad, but they were not. For some reason, I am drawn to an artist in his final years, and Buster is no exception. I think of Orson Welles, white haired and heavy, chain smoking cigars, desperately trying to get money together for doomed film projects while critics and filmmakers put his Citizen Kane, released forty years earlier I might add, up on a pedestal. He wrestled with an intimidating youth, a reputation he could not live up to, while appearing in wine adverts and popping up in films unworthy of his talent, but to which the great man gave a touch of class with little effort.

I think of Salvador Dali, who in his final years holed himself up in his castle, a spent artist of yesteryear, a parody of his former self, far and away from the prying eyes of the world, as his people ran around after him seeing to his business and making the best deals they could. Like many genius artists of film, art and music, he had become a product, a shadow of the once exuberant icon, a business. Many great men end up this way, with their ego too large to move on and accept an immovable destiny, and their own mortality to boot.

Keaton's final era is more humble, but also much less depressing. He was still working up to his dying month, and the man seemed to have reached a psychologically healthy place in his life - finally, it has to be said. His films were finding new audiences, and even as the praise and plaudits came upon him, Keaton was pleasantly surprised by his newfound adoration, not acting as if it was what was expected and precisely what he deserved. This ego-less star persisted and kept his eye on the tracks, looking for the next job and challenge, the next gag, the next pay off and pay cheque.

This book explores, in various essays and articles, the merits of Keaton's final era, the two-reelers, the experiments, the guest roles and the re-emergence of his classic work. I am looking at an artist who made his most acclaimed work 90 to 100 years ago, who died half a century ago and whose influence seems to grow as time marches on. This is a look at the final years, and days, in the life and work of Buster Keaton, in my view the true genius of the silent era.

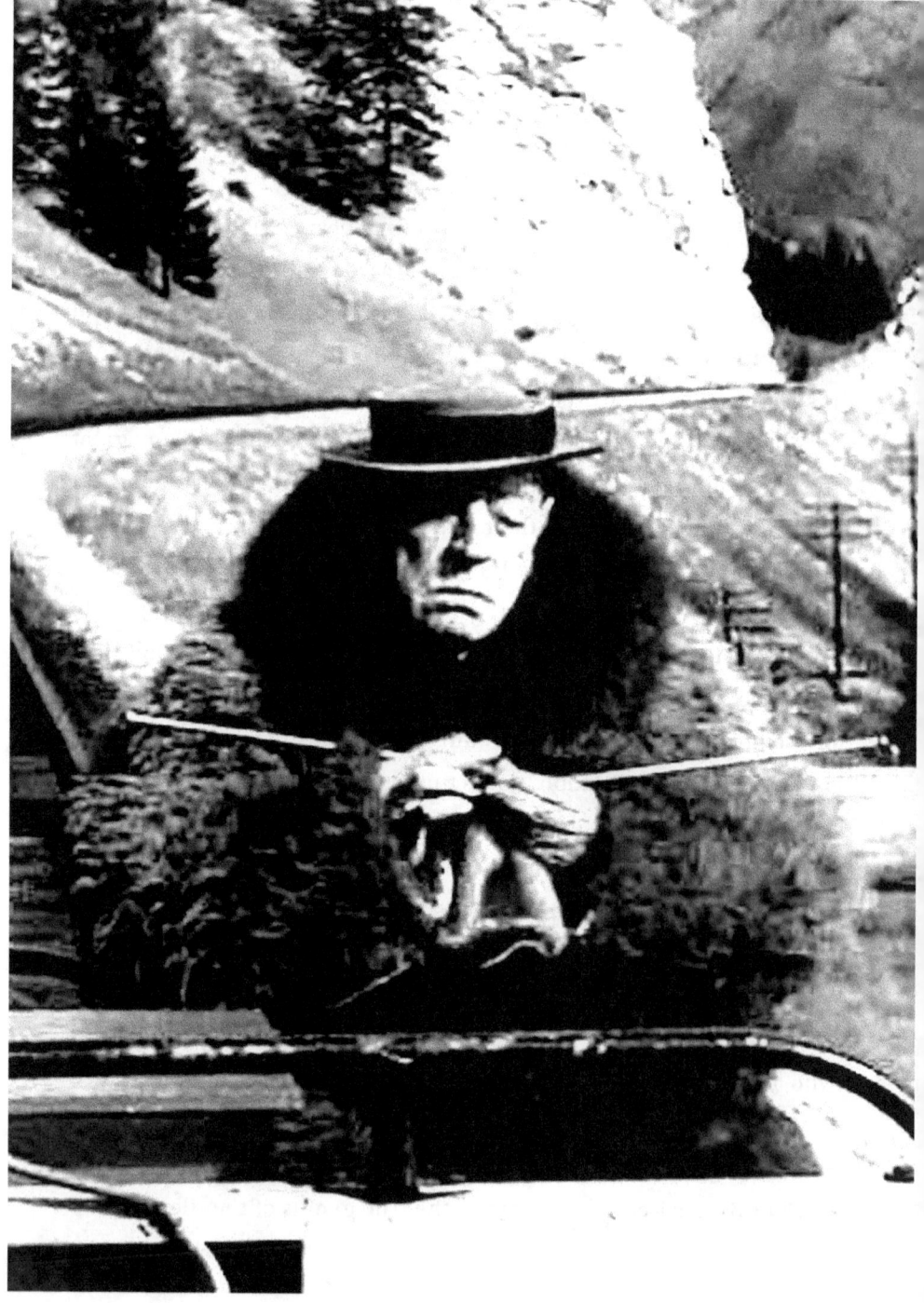

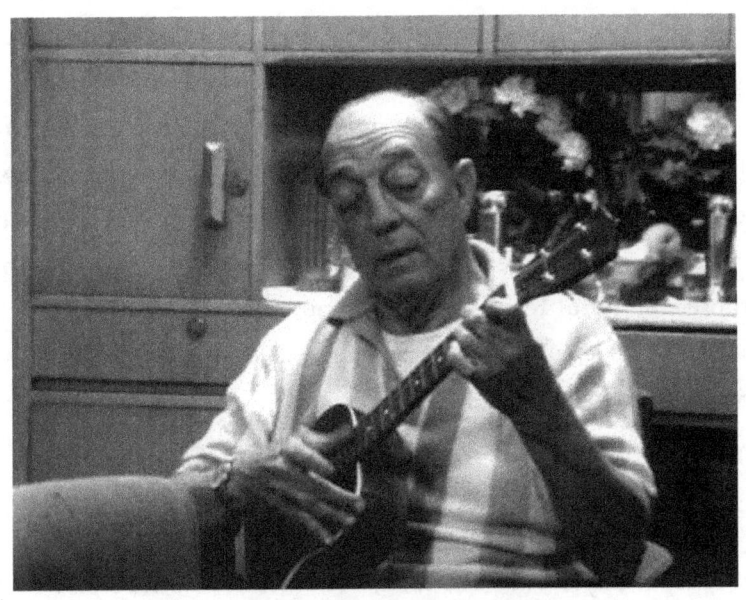

LOOKING BACK

The Ups and Downs of Buster Keaton's Film Career

""My first salaried week was in 1899. I have completed sixty one years." - Buster Keaton, 1960

In 1964, silent film historian Kevin Brownlow paid a visit to Buster Keaton's modest home in Woodland Hills, California, an abode Brownlow describes as a change from his earlier, more famous luxury home, which was then owned by actor James Mason. Keaton had been a rich man, but lost it all in a divorce years earlier. Another failed marriage had followed, and some troubled times indeed; but now, in his late sixties, Keaton had been with the love of his life for twenty odd years, the great Eleanor, a former MGM dancer he fell in love with back in 1940.

In the introduction to his interview with Buster, Brownlow brilliantly described his first sighting of the ageing film veteran, a "short, stout elderly man; the light was behind him, so I couldn't see his face. Then he stepped into close-up, and I caught my first glimpse of those wonderful features. Keaton had a voice like an anchor chain running out. He had a very expressive face, even when supposedly deadpan, but in reality he laughed a lot."

One can only envy Brownlow, standing before the icon himself in his home, in the closing chapter of his own saga. Buster had lived a life, and you could tell that by looking at him. Though still fit as a fiddle, especially for an old man, the lines on his face told us he'd been through the meat grinder, but the twinkle in his eyes suggested he'd come out a wise man. In the piece, Brownlow goes on to describe a talkative Buster, delighting in his memories and long forgotten anecdotes about the making of his movies, the recollections of which brought laughter into the room. This paints a wonderful picture of the aged Buster, a man in love with living, very much in the present (at the time of this interview he was on standby with a film studio who might have needed his presence at any time), but more than happy to regal with tales of old. The icon once forgotten and sidelined by the film industry was coming back in a big way, and he was loving every second of it.

The image of a cosy Buster in the mid 1960s is harshly contrasted against his younger years, especially his infancy, which he spent on the stage with his parents as part of a performing act. Of course, any old man would notice the juxtaposition of his current life with his formative days, but Buster's seemed all the more remarkable due to the journey he had been on in between. By the "in between" part, I mean crafting (hand crafting in fact) some of the finest pictures ever made, in his glory years, the roaring twenties, going through a dip in the thirties and forties, and enjoying a revival in his favour during the fifties and sixties.

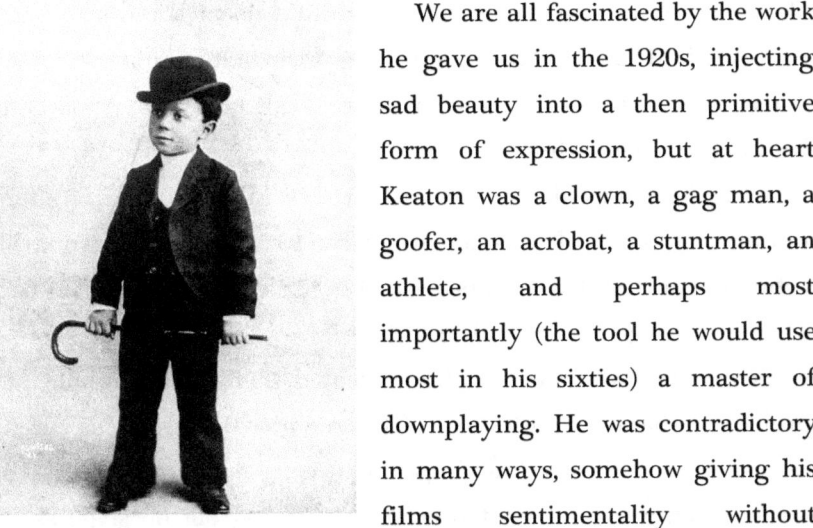

We are all fascinated by the work he gave us in the 1920s, injecting sad beauty into a then primitive form of expression, but at heart Keaton was a clown, a gag man, a goofer, an acrobat, a stuntman, an athlete, and perhaps most importantly (the tool he would use most in his sixties) a master of downplaying. He was contradictory in many ways, somehow giving his films sentimentality without manipulating the viewer, getting our sympathy without making himself a sympathetic character and staying subtly true, even when he was hanging off buildings and fast moving trains. But the roots of this genius were established years before he hit the big screen.

Like all the great screen stars of the early 20th century, Buster Keaton's performing life began on the vaudeville stage. He was born Joseph Frank Keaton in October of 1895, in Piqua, Kansas, the location where the family happened to have stopped while travelling the country with their stage act. In a 1921 interview, Keaton said "the place where I was born isn't there any more. It was in Kansas, and shortly after I arrived, there was a cyclone that demolished the place. They never did build it up."

Keaton's childhood is the stuff of legend, so extraordinary it sounds fabricated, but of course is not. His dad, Joseph Keaton Sr., ran a show with the one and only Harry Houdini, where they sold medicine on the side. Buster got his nickname, reportedly, when Houdini saw the youngster take a tumble down some stairs, and exclaimed, "That's a Buster", meaning a notable tumble. "That's a good name," said Keaton's old man, "we'll call him that." Apparently, he was only 18 months old at the time.

When he was a baby, Buster was once left in a costume trunk for a number of hours. The incident nearly suffocated him. To avoid future death risks, his parents decided to leave the young Buster back at the boarding house while they performed. However, as soon as Buster could walk and talk, he presented them with a whole new problem - what to do with Buster. The true pros they were, his parents had a solution. By the mere age of three, Buster joined in on his family's act, with mother, father and son going out on stage as the Three Keatons.

"Oh, a kid born backstage," he told Herbert Feinstein in 1960, "the parents slap makeup on him as soon as he can walk... sometimes just for the fun of it, and their own amusement, and also to see if the kid takes to an audience at a young age."

It sounds like a rather surreal act; the mother played saxophone on the side, while Buster and his old man did the main performing. Most of the routine consisted of Buster misbehaving, and his dad throwing him around the stage as punishment. Even in the late 19th century, these kind of goings on were rather shocking, and officials were often called out to check Buster wasn't being mistreated, as allegations of child abuse were being thrown around (no pun intended) the place. The act was so physical for Buster (rumour has it that his dad once threw Buster into the audience, aiming him at a rather irritating and relentless heckler) that his body got used to the blows, ensuring that for the rest of his days he would be able to fall gracefully without (mostly) doing himself any serious damage. "They don't hurt," he once said of his falls and stunts. "Great Scott, if they did, they'd kill me off. It's all in knowing how to take the fall. It isn't nearly as difficult as it looks."

In what was dubbed "The Roughest Act That Was Ever in the History of the Stage", Buster was billed as "The Little Boy Who Can't Be Damaged", unbelievable in today's climate. That said, this hard life gave Keaton thick skin, bendable bones, and plenty of valuable experience. His alcoholic father may have been a little too hard on him, but the apprenticeship served him well. When his parents were arrested and Buster had to be stripped and searched for bruises however, it was clear that the Keatons may have been taking things a little too far. And whether he really did only attend one day of school or not (rumour has it his only schooling day was in New York while the family act was working there, and even that was only a part of a day), the "fact" added more mystery to the Keaton myth.

"My old man was an eccentric comic and as soon as I could take care of myself at all on my feet, he had slapshoes on me and big baggy pants," Buster later recalled. "And he'd just start doing gags with me and especially kickin' me clean across the stage or taking me by the back of the neck and throwing me."

Buster wasn't going to be a boy forever though, and the family act's days were numbered. How much longer could his dad get away with this? It was time for him to spread his wings. Keaton began to get a name for himself, even venturing over to the UK for a tour of vaudeville theatres. When his dad's alcoholism became too much to bare, Buster and his mother left and ended up in New York, leaving the old man behind in California. It was here that Buster's attention turned to the screen, an art form still in its primitive infancy to a certain degree, at least on a narrative level. After a stint on Broadway in Passing Show through 1917, Keaton stumbled into the medium that was to become his main obsession until the end of his life.

Though his father looked down on films, and indeed Buster himself had some reservations about them himself, he instantly fell in love with the world of cinema. But with so much competition trying to get into the lucrative and well exposed industry, how would Keaton get himself noticed?

Keaton found a way. His first film appearance came in 1917, 101 years ago at the time of writing, with a co-starring role in the Roscoe "Fatty" Arbuckle picture, The Butcher Boy. While working in the theatre, Buster ran into an old friend who happened to be strolling along in toe with Arbuckle, by chance (a spot of luck, if we are going by Keaton's version of events) meeting one of the biggest film stars of the time. Roscoe had been appointed by producer Joseph Schenck to write and direct (and star in, obviously) a string of two-reelers, and as long as he did eight a year, he was doing OK. Obviously aware of Keaton's talent, Arbuckle cast him in The Butcher Boy.

"Roscoe asked me if I had ever been in a motion picture," Buster told Film Quarterly in 1958. "I said no I hadn't even been in a studio.

He said come on down to the studio Monday and do a scene with me and see how you like it. I went down there and I worked in it. That scene is in the finished picture and instead of doing just a bit he carried me the whole way through it. I was very interested in the mechanics of it. I wanted to know how the picture got put together..."

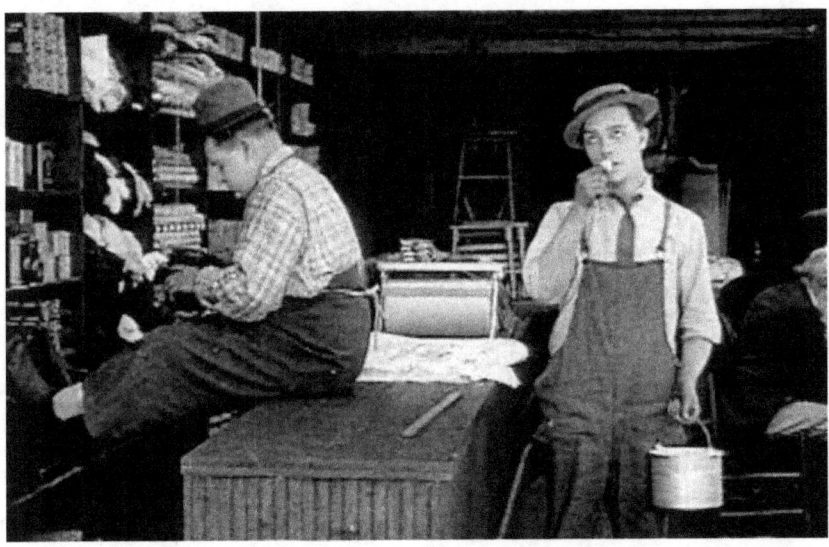

The quickie has Arbuckle as a butcher worker who falls for the daughter of the store's manager, Mr Grouch. (Alice Lake plays the object of his desire.) Buster's brief part comes to life when he gets involved in the middle of Arbuckle's scrap with a love rival, played by Al St. John. Even at such an early stage, Buster sticks out from the other players, even Roscoe, who is admittedly fabulous. In fact the two work wonderfully together, and are a nice little double act even from their first film together.

Buster has some great moments in The Butcher Boy, surely one of the best debuts of the silent era. He shows his masterful grip on comic timing and foolery; such as when he butts in on the chess game, when Arbuckle lifts him up on to the counter by the back of his pants, when he glues his own hat to his head, and perhaps best of all, gets hit face on by a bag of flour. It's interesting to watch The Butcher Boy again, side by side with the likes of The Railrodder, and even the lesser later two-reelers, like The Triumph of Lester Snapwell and The Scribe, all released in the 1960s. One notices, quite simply, how so little changed in Buster's delivery and mechanics. All those decades on, he could fall the same way, even as an old man.

Unlike many silent screen stars of this age, Buster leapt forward in the space of one single picture. Though you wouldn't think it could be possible in only a matter of months, the juxtaposition between the Keaton of The Butcher Boy and the one who comes glowing off the screen in The Rough House is simply staggering. The Butcher Boy had been directed by Arbuckle, and as he was the central figure in it, few of the rest of the cast were given close ups or serious coverage. Indeed, Keaton himself was just a supporting player, hence why he was only ever shot from a distance alongside the others. In Rough House though, in which Keaton got to experience actually directing alongside the film's main star Roscoe Arbuckle, Buster is up front and in your face, already on his way to world stardom.

What separated Keaton from the large number of silent screen comics on the rise in this era was his serious ambition to be a director. Like Chaplin and Arbuckle, he wasn't interested in a screen career unless he could have the control. Keaton had been fascinated by the inner workings of the motion picture camera, had wanted to understand the process, and how to get the best results out of the device. From The Rough House onwards, the legendary Buster Keaton was learning more and more about his craft.

It's easy to see how hilarious these shorts would have been back in the day, and Arbuckle is a genuinely funny clown. However, though the chaotic shenanigans hold the interest, we are still firmly in the territory of Keystone Cops (Mack Sennett's farcical short film company, which released movies between 1912 and 17, as well as starting the film careers of Roscoe and Charlie Chaplin respectively) than anything matching the beauty and scope of the likes of The Navigator or The General. Buster's masterpieces were a few years away just yet, but in the meantime, those lucky enough to be journeying through his filmography can sit back and enjoy the delights of the Arbuckle era.

Despite the two great openers, the best Keaton/Arbuckle work was yet to come. For me, His Wedding Night is perhaps the funniest and most accomplished Arbuckle/Keaton co starrer out there. Again directed by Arbuckle, it stars Al St. John and Roscoe as rivals for the heart of Alice Mann. There are the usual smattering of visual gags, falls and in this case melon throwing, but there is also the added bonus of seeing delivery boy Keaton in a dress, and getting mistaken for Alice, before being kidnapped by Al. Crammed full of neat little visual jokes (Arbuckle changing the price of the gas when an expensive car comes up), it's very much the Arbuckle show, but Buster threatens to steal this one right from under his nose.

Coney Island was another Arbuckle feature with a supporting turn by Buster, released in October of the same year, only in this one he appears on screen first within the first minute. Keaton is seen enjoying the Mardi Gras Parade - or attempting to anyway, seeing as he and his sweetheart can't see over the punter's heads. In the end Keaton climbs a lamp post, claps and smiles in glee and then comes tumbling down. Avid viewers may note Keaton's range of emotion too, and his wonderful scenes at the fun fair. He hadn't yet decided that total stoniness was the key to his success.

Coney Island has become one of the most celebrated early films to feature Buster, and he often spoke of its creation. In interviews, however, Keaton downplayed the complexities and hard work involved in making such a short two-reeler come to life and work as a

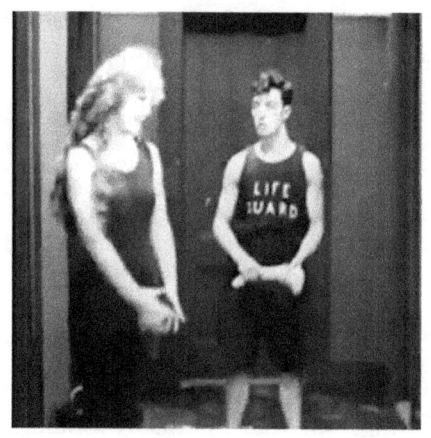

stand alone film. "I remember making it very well," he said of Coney Island. "Nothing to write about. We just went down there, went on all the concessions at Luna Park and got in trouble - that was all there was to that."

Keaton always spoke about his life's work as if it were nothing. He was humble and modest, but by not bigging himself up and exposing the skill that went into the early shorts, he made them seem somehow more magic, as if God himself blessed these men and gave them their talent fully formed. He did however comment to Kevin Brownlow that he thought Arbuckle was one of the great filmmakers of that era, and noted how their difference in size and expressiveness made their partnership what it was. However, when he claimed that Fatty's grin contrasted with Buster's own blank, emotionless demeanour, Brownlow could not help but point out the several smiles and titters of these early collaborations, such as the laugh in Coney Island. Maybe, Keaton might have considered, that the classic Buster screen persona was still being defined and refined.

Out West was a leap not only for Arbuckle, and to a lesser extent Keaton too, but for the whole two-reeler format, and arguably for where and what cinema was at that point. A blatant satire on the western genre, the film might sting a little in some segments (such as when Arbuckle tries to booze up the Salvation Army girl and they torture and torment the black man), but in context of the time it was made, it's perfectly fine, especially as it's ribbing the twisted morals of the western genre. Here, film has become self aware for the first time, and it doesn't mind poking fun at itself.

For his part, Keaton is fabulous as the town sheriff, first seen at the saloon bar curing an eye problem with a shot of firewater. Somehow, in the old worldly setting, familiar set ups and often eerily old fashioned feel, Keaton sticks out as something truly special, a face from another time; perhaps as Ebert called him, a visitor from another age paying the silent era a visit. He is brilliant in Out West, comically spot on and also providing the film with a fair amount of creepy moments too; whenever someone dies, Keaton kicks him aside and rolls him into a trap door, then covers it up. There is a definitive shift in tone (it's much darker actually), and the film feels more carefully worked out. The fact it was a co write with Keaton's wife Natalie Talmadge explains a lot, and maybe her influence rubbed off on Arbuckle in the visual department too, for it looks better than the previous shorts.

There are other stand outs too. Released in March of 1918, The Bell Boy is among the best known works of Arbuckle, in which he and Keaton play bellboys at the Elk's Head Hotel. Keaton was to later recycle much of the material for later starring vehicles, but in the crusty confines of the Arbuckle short, they work brilliantly. At this stage it is clear that Arbuckle is relying on Keaton's physicality more and more, and if I am going to be honest, as great as Roscoe is, he is starting to be outshone by Buster. Observing Keaton's speedy progression into a fully rounded clown and film star in his own right, there is little wonder he was catapulted into stardom so quickly.

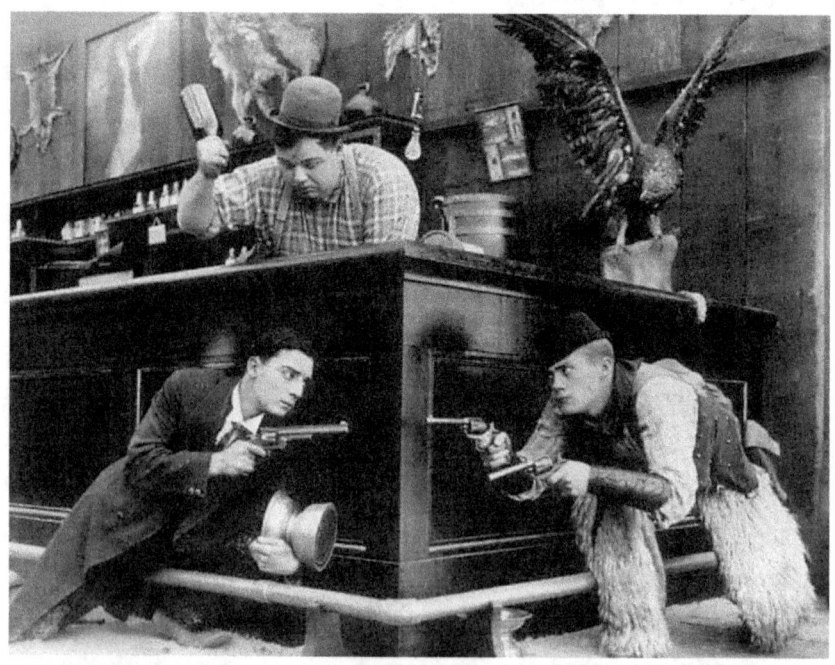

In The Bell Boy, Keaton presents his unique and seemingly impossible skill at throwing himself around in all manner of unbelievable ways, and not "seriously" hurting himself in the process. This is iconic Keaton territory, and for my book the first truly remarkable work he did. The classic phone booth "window cleaning" scene alone is worth the price of admission, but one can only gasp in awe at the way he launches himself over the hotel counter, gets casually pushed off the desk by Arbuckle (notice Keaton's gleeful smile as he plays pat-a-cake with Roscoe and Rasputin the Mystic) and doesn't seem to mind his head being repeatedly trapped in the elevator door.

By now, Keaton has become utterly magnetic on screen, and it's fair to say that you can't keep your eyes off him. In this rapid run of two-reelers, some being less remarkable than others, The Cook is definitely something special, and Keaton gets to step out front in what is surely one of the finest short comedies from the early 20th century, pre-1920, when the likes of Chaplin. Harold Lloyd and Keaton were really getting going.

Anyone accustomed to the straight-faced (stone faced, that should say) Buster of The General et al. may find the lightness of his Arbuckle collaborations as something of a breeze. Clearly, Buster had not yet honed his persona, and he was happy to play second fiddle to a true master of his time. On the blog Sister Celluloid, the writer nailed it when they wrote of Buster and Arbuckle's shorts, and The Cook in general: "If you first fell in love with Buster Keaton in the films he wrote and directed himself, seeing his early two-reelers with Fatty is a bit like stumbling across old home movies of your dad as a teenager, goofing around in the basement with his friends. Before he had any real responsibilities. Before anyone was looking."

And that's exactly how it feels to me, as someone more familiar with the maverick auteur genius of the twenties. He is fast, loose and care free here, and I love every minute of it. That said, it was only a matter of time before Keaton would tire of being Arbuckle's right hand man. Like Chaplin enduring his way through the Keystone Cop movies because he knew it was the only way to get starring/directorial work and full control, Keaton not so much endured his Roscoe collaborations (he clearly enjoys himself throughout) but got through them. The great thing of course is that they are all - but one, the lost Country Hero being an irritating absentee - easy to view, and one can see Buster's progression as they go along. The Cook features some wonderful Keaton mayhem (the waiting scenes are terrific) and it should not be overlooked as simply "another" Arbuckle/Keaton short, at least not in my view. Lost for years, it was rediscovered in 1998, and fully restored in the 21st century. It was also his last short before he embarked on his World War 2 service.

Though Keaton missed combat in the war, he did get involved in a spot of bother nonetheless. "Late one night I had a narrow escape while coming back from a card game," he later recalled. "A sentry challenged me, and I didn't hear his demand for the password or the two warnings he gave me after that. Then he pulled back the breech of his gun, prepared to shoot. My life was saved by my sixth sense which enabled me to hear that gun click – and stopped me dead in my tracks."

With his uniform hung up in the wardrobe, and his life intact, Keaton was welcomed back by his friend Arbuckle, and the pair set about making another film together; again, directed by Roscoe. Back Stage is unique in the Arbuckle/Keaton shorts, because it has them working in the magical - or here not so magical - world of show business. Rather than being performers though, they are behind the scenes men, painting sets and moving things around. However, when the main performers refuse to do their show, Roscoe and Buster end up on stage. At one point they are even dragged up, and though the show is a mess, they get a round of applause from the viewers, who assume that all the failings were deliberate. It ends in a highly dramatic fashion, for an Arbuckle film at least, involving a shoot out and a box of weights landing on the strongman's head.

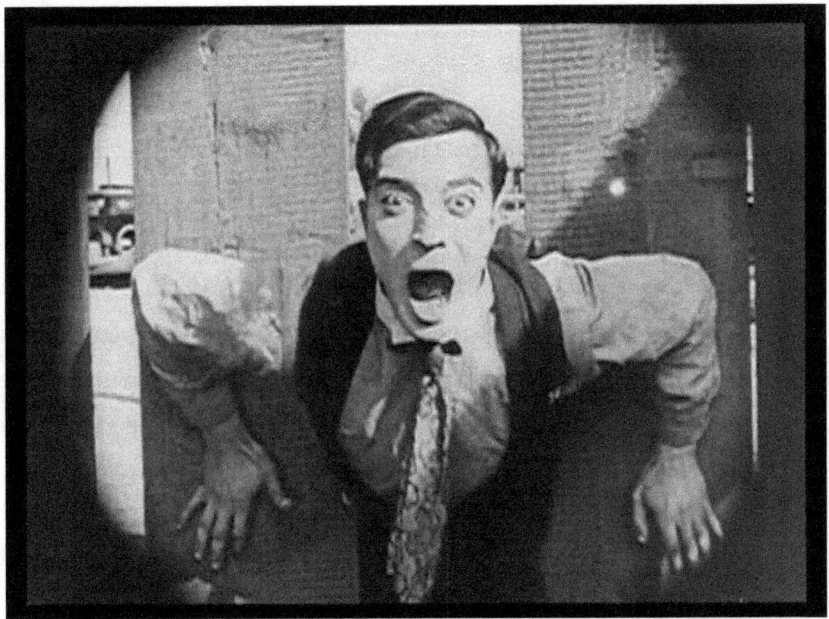

The Garage was the final Keaton/Arbuckle short, very much the end of an era, and the duo went out together in style. They play two guys working at a fire station/car garage, and ironically with it being their last film, they play more of a duo/team than they do in earlier films. Without romantic sub plots, the pair get to clown around together more freely, and the results are fabulous. A pity, then, that this was to be their final collaboration.

As much as the pair work well together, there is a feeling that Arbuckle wanted to give Keaton more screen time to prepare him and viewers for the full-on Buster experience to come in the rest of the 1920s. Littered with stand out comic gems, for me the highlight is the wonderful scene when Buster gets caught in the fence and has his rear end bitten by a dog. The shot of him, face to camera (breaking the fourth wall again) and screaming in agony is a joy to behold, and remains the defining image (in my view) of Keaton's time with Roscoe. This is a vital film, bridging the important gap between his role as a sidekick/sideman to a fully fledged leading star in his own right, the transition, thanks to The Garage, seems kind of seamless. Keaton took to lead acting naturally.

But the truth is that Buster outgrew the strict limitations of two-reeler comedies as a sideman, and went on to sign a contract for solo films; as did Arbuckle, after years of Keystone clunkers and short starring roles. However, tragedy struck, which put an end to the frolics and good fun of Arbuckle's reign. Only a year after their last film together, Arbuckle became entangled in a seedy controversy where he was put on trial for the murder of a woman at a party. Virginia Rappe had been suffering from cystitis, which was worsened by her excessive alcohol abuse. After being taken ill at Roscoe's hotel room (he was having a party at his suite, but had already gone to bed to rest as the shenanigans continued), she went to the hospital with Bambina Delmont, who claimed her friend had been raped by Roscoe. When Rappe died, Arbuckle was arrested for her murder. As they saw it, his size must have caused her bladder to rupture during this alleged forced act of sex. Though eventually acquitted and found innocent of the crime, the incident ruined his career. As Roscoe's fame declined rapidly, Keaton's was on the rise. Buster spoke out for Arbuckle's innocence, only once in fact, but he was reprimanded by the studio for displaying loyalty to his old friend. Even in its earliest years, there was an ugly rot in the centre of the Hollywood machine that could not be excused.

Roscoe's treatment was truly awful, and given that he was definitely one of the finest clowns of the silent era, it is a tragedy that the crime he did not even commit has over shadowed much of his work. Arbuckle's fall coincided with Keaton's rise, and the great genius clown whose only true artistic rival was Charlie Chaplin (Harold Lloyd was just as popular, though his films as pieces of filmmaking were not as praised) was given his turn in the spotlight. And though many might overlook these Arbuckle pictures merely as Buster's three year screen apprenticeship, there is a lot more to them than simply being a platform for a comic learning his trade; these are noteworthy classics in their own right. Though creaky in parts, there are enough moments of mini magic to ensure they remain a vital part of Buster's on screen work, and the silent film canon in general.

Though there is plenty of Buster Keaton madness and magic to enjoy in the Arbuckle years of 1917 to 1920, Keaton only truly came into his own as a mega star and master of the screen at the turn of the 1920s, when Joseph Schenck decided to give Keaton his own starring vehicles. "He bought me Chaplin's old studio, and named it the Keaton studio," Buster said in 1960. "All he did as producer, he says, 'You're to make eight two-reelers a year we're going to release through Metro,' so Schenck never knew when I was shooting, or what I was shooting."

Between 1920 and 1923, Keaton made 19 short two-reelers which help establish him as the legendary Great Stone Face of the silver screen, as well one feature length movie released in October of 1920, The Saphead. It is a truly remarkable run of work, only matched in this era, in my view at least, by Keaton's blazing ream of classic features he made between the years 1923 to 1928.

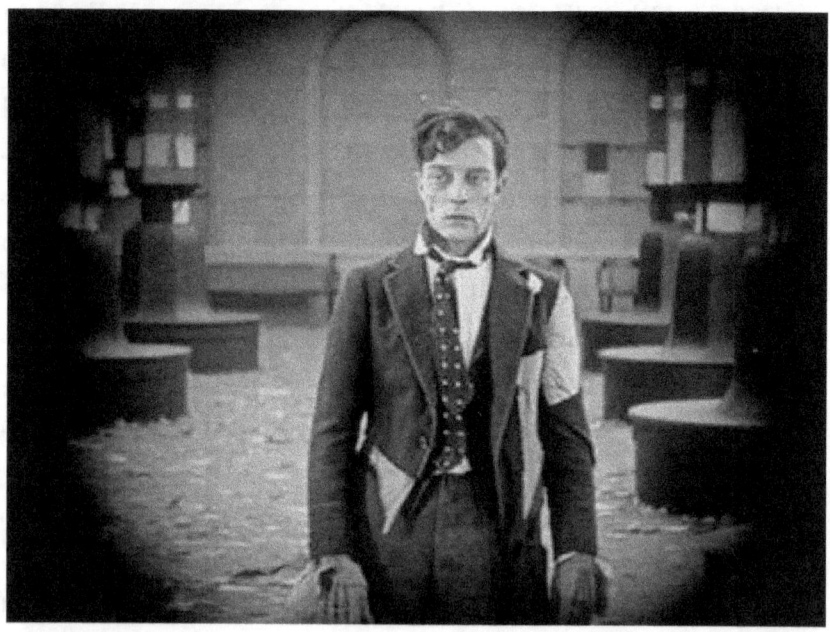

Firstly though he appeared in The Saphead, based on the play The New Henrietta, which had starred Douglas Fairbanks, the very man who recommended Buster for the film version. Buster plays Bertie, a party animal and excessive gambler, son of Nicholas Van Alstyne, the richest man in New York City. It turns out that Bertie is not the drunken oaf he portrays himself to be, and is in fact acting this way in a hope to win the affection of Agnes (Beulah Booker), his adopted sister. What follows is a series of events, resulting in Bertie accidentally saving the family's fortune and finally marrying his sweetheart, with whom he has twin children. A happily ever after ensues...

Directed by Herbert Blache and Winchell Smith, it runs for 77 minutes and just about keeps the attention, though it often sags a little. One cannot help but wonder what kind of picture we would have if Buster been given the chance to direct it. Firstly, he would have more than likely snipped it down to a leaner length and tightened the slacker areas. Still, even if you are challenged by its slow pace, and more serious general tone (at least for a Keaton movie) The Saphead itself is notable for being Buster's first full length feature. As far as Buster goes, The Saphead is rather good, and in the wake of his Arbuckle shorts, it shows that Keaton could carry a full story himself (mostly), and also gain empathy and adoration from the audience without presenting himself as an overly sentimental character. His Bertie is a true creation, flawed but likeable, and a prototype anti-hero in the truest sense. There is an element of Flashman about him too (the cad reinvented by George MacDonald Fraser from Thomas Hughes' Tom Brown's School Days), but Bertie is very much classic embryonic Keaton.

"A film comedy is assembled with the same precision as the inner working of a watch..."

Though his earlier work had its charm, as flawed as it often was, One Week is no doubt Keaton's first bona fide masterpiece. Directed by Keaton with Edward F. Cline (and written by the pair too), it runs for a lean 19 minutes and today remains a classic of the two-reeler silent era. It's remarkable that when they did give Keaton the controls and let him steer the camera and point it exactly where he wanted to, the results were so undeniably good from the word go.

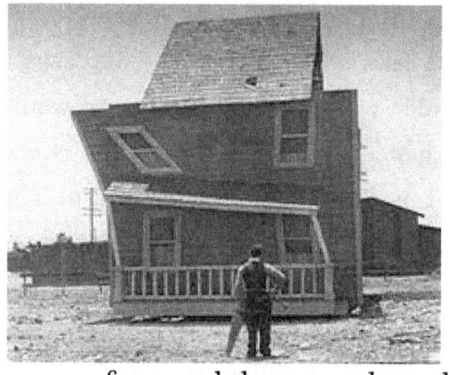 This, in many ways, is the true beginning of the Buster Keaton story. Seeing him goof around with Arbuckle is one thing, and is perfectly enjoyable too, but this feels like the first stepping stone on a path of development (a career of ups and downs, peaks and troughs) that ends in the mid 1960s, nearly fifty years later.

Keaton had in fact already directed a film himself, The High Sign, but Buster thought it was too weak to debut with, so left it back a year and quickly made One Week instead. As it goes, it was one of the wisest choices a filmmaker ever made. Starting with a simple premise of a newlywed couple (Buster and Sybil Seely, a charming couple if there ever was one) getting a flat pack, build-it-yourself house as a wedding present, the film unfolds (no pun intended) into a work of comic genius, with stunning visual set pieces coming one after the other. Keaton had seen a Ford Motor film called Home Made (filmed the previous year) which educated on self assembled homes, and decided to poke fun at it, just as he and Roscoe had done with the western genre in Out West. But One Week is so much sharper than anything he did with Roscoe, existing as both hilarious comic entertainment and a parody of married life, and the pressures of setting up a successful home life, and, quite literally, a home.

Technically, One Week still looks stunning, and what makes it more special is that the amazing visuals were done physically in a plain and straight forward way. If they made One Week today it could all be achieved - soullessly I might add - with the aid of CGI special effects. But as this was 1920, Keaton and the crew only had one option - to do it as the viewer sees it. Alas, the house was built on a turntable, the train sequence was shot for real (no model work here folks) and Buster risked his life throughout for real. In fact, he genuinely hurt himself during filming the scene when he falls down two stories (Keaton suffered back and limb injuries), and clearly learnt from the experience to be a little more careful in the future.

From a modern viewer's perspective, every single shot of One Week is perfection, or at least close to it. From its opening line about the sourness of the initially sweet sounding wedding bells, the first shot of the said bells ringing out, Keaton and wife leaving church and being driven home in their Just Married car, Keaton establishes himself as a filmmaker of class. Every set up is superbly chosen, and the framing is excellent. Clearly, Keaton learned a lot from being a part of the 14 Arbuckle shorts (and to a lesser extent, the Saphead feature, perhaps on what *not* to do, rather than what to do) and he excels as director. Every sequence is a touch of genius (the early car swap is still breathtaking, especially when Buster is swept off by the motorcycle) and it's evident that Keaton has carefully considered every set up, every scene, every gag, every second it seems. Buster is the very definition of a filmmaker, conscious of every facet of the art of the motion picture.

It is in the house assemblage sequences where Buster truly becomes the awe-inspiring clown we all know and love, and even though he is poking fun at the pressures of married life, there is also a lot of affection here. Buster's character desperately wants to make things right for him and his new wife, but that dastardly rival (played by Joe Roberts) is sure to sabotage the whole thing. It's funny yes, but on a purely visual level the whole thing is hard to fathom. The way the house swizzles round, falls on him (the classic scene we all know and love, where he is saved by the window frame), gets taken on wheels (looking like it's about to collapse into pieces before our eyes) and ultimately gets hit by the train still stuns me to this day. It leads me to believe that, in retrospect, Keaton achieved perfection in his directorial works more than any other silent auteur of the era, Chaplin included. One Week is a masterpiece, short, sweet and utterly unforgettable, establishing Keaton as the genius of the short form. For me, it is also stylistically linked to his later work, perhaps more so than any other early picture, making it an essential piece of study.

Convict 13, again a collaboration with writer-director Eddie Cline, was another quickie comedy with some decent gags and set ups, all shot through the eye (or should that be eyes) of a filmmaker who knew what he wanted. Yes he was aided by Cline, but Keaton was in charge. Two films into his self directing career and Buster was still learning. While Convict 13 is a nice film, and certainly influential (we see shades of it in early Woody Allen), it feels somewhat shabbier, messier even, than One Week and some of his later, more polished works. Still, as a speedy knockabout comedy, it hits the spot, and would cheer almost anyone up after a bad day.

If anything though, if one is viewing it in context of Keaton's development, it feels like a considerable step backwards. One Week had been a sharp, witty, sympathetic and magical satire of married life and the pressures it entails, but Convict 13 feels more flat; funny yes, of course it is, but it's also certainly rather one dimensional. But one has to be realistic and admit that this film is 98 years old, and at the time will have been hilarious, exciting and multi faceted. Judging it to Buster's finest work makes it look rather creaky, and dare I say it, more crude. Still, there are some fabulous scenes that any true Buster fan will enjoy. For instance, the failed hanging sequence is classic Keaton; the opening golf ball segment is what made Buster the premier inept clown of the day (trying extra hard to do something which, from the outside, seems rather facile) and should not be overlooked; while the closing riot (with gun fire and all) comes as something of a surprise, being one of the most violent sequences I have seen in any silent comedy. Special note must go to Joe Roberts, Buster's resident heavy, smacking the guard with the sledge hammer.

Neighbors, also released in 1920 and a collaboration with Cline, is right up there with Buster's finest two-reelers. It's tight, funny, well structured, superbly acted, wonderfully performed, full of daring Buster stunts and has a tidy little ending to make it all worthwhile.

Buster and Virginia Fox play a couple living in opposing grubby tenements, whose families constantly quarrel and bicker over their young romance. Like Romeo and Juliet, their love is doomed, and neither family wants it to blossom. Joe Roberts plays the girl's dad, who seems to relish and delight in beating the stuffing out of Buster, and in one of the film's best scenes, tying him to the washing line and catapulting him back home. After a court case deems Buster legally within his rights to marry her, the family feud continues at the wedding, and she is dragged home by her dad when it becomes known that Buster intends to give her a 10 cent ring. In the end,

Buster gets the girl (in the most physically impressive way possible) and they are married by a blacksmith... only in Keaton's world could that last sentence be a reality.

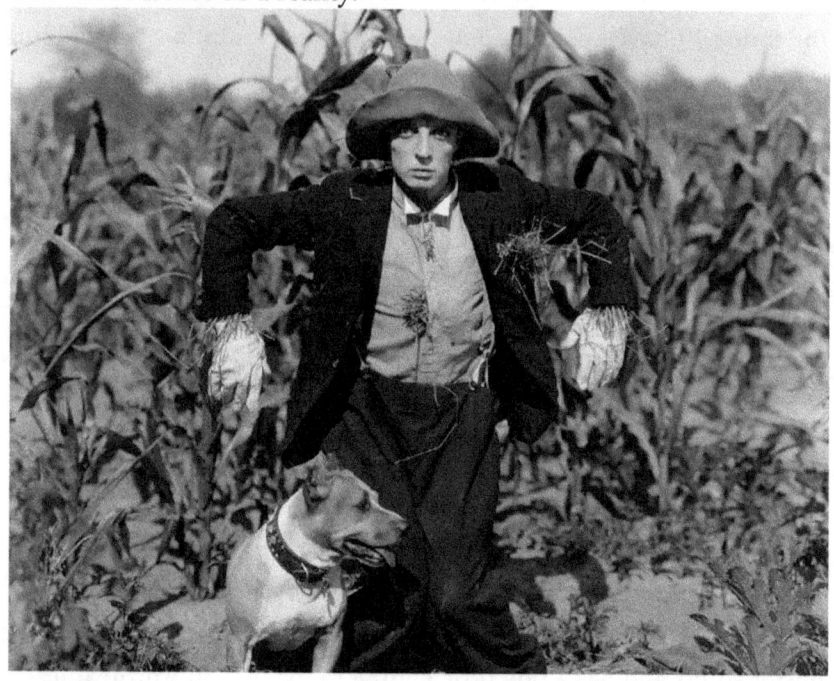

By now, Buster had the luxury of his own studio, and was becoming a big star. His pictures were successful, and the critics loved him too. Chaplin was on the cusp of making features at this point (The Kid would be released one year later), thus moving into a league all of his own; but in his own right, Buster's status was high in 1920. Seeing the work he was doing from a modern perspective, nearly 100 years on, it's clear to see why. Looking back, Neighbors is as close to perfect as a 20 minute comedy could get back in the 1920s. The supporting cast fit their roles like gloves, and Buster, here in his mid twenties, is at the top of his game. His comic timing is impeccable and his physicality truly spellbinding. Buster's glow aside, it's also remarkable how little Neighbors has dated, and how funny it still is. In fact, it's far funnier than most modern comedy, and seems much more pure and true in many ways. The pace is fast, the jokes are plenty, and the direction is brilliant.

Keaton's last short of 1920 was The Scarecrow, another winner which features Buster as a farm worker who is after the heart of the farmer's daughter, played by Sybil Seely. He has a rival, though, in Keaton regular Joe Roberts, and a seemingly rabid dog (played by Luke the Dog, who belonged to Roscoe Arbuckle and featured in quite a few silent comedies) who wants his blood. When fleeing the hound, Keaton's clothes are torn and ruined, so he takes the garments from a nearby scarecrow. After a misunderstanding, the farmer's daughter believes Buster is proposing to her, and they are wed while sitting on a motorcycle.

The film does feel rather like a throwback to the Roscoe/Buster shorts, but it has enough of its own stand out moments to justify its singularity and make it one of my personal favourites. The chase scene with the dog is undeniably brilliant (Luke is just as impressive as Buster it has to be said; just watch him scale that ladder), and how Keaton is so clearly risking his life on the battered walls of the old farm building makes your toes curl. The best moment for me is when Buster thinks he's escaped from the pursuing dog and lights himself a cigarette, only to realise the dog is still after him. The chase continues, taking up quite a large chunk of the movie in fact, until they shake on it and make friends. It's a joyous film. My only complaint is that I would have loved to have seen more scenes with Buster as the Scarecrow, as his nimble athleticism would have adapted wonderfully to the rag doll physicality a Scarecrow might have. Still, how can you not get a thrill from the scene where Buster, disguised as the Scarecrow, winds Roberts and the farmer up by kicking them both up the arse, and then gets chased through the corn?

Buster's run of silent comedy shorties ran until 1923, taking in such highlights as The Electric House (1922), The Blacksmith (also 1922, and viciously underrated in my view), and his final two-reeler from this era, 1923's The Love Nest, before he branched out into features and that run of undeniable, immortal classics.

Three Ages (1923) and Our Hospitality (1923) are the beginning of this uninterrupted run, where Keaton was at the wheel, in control of the movies he was making, and his own destiny to boot. He was a 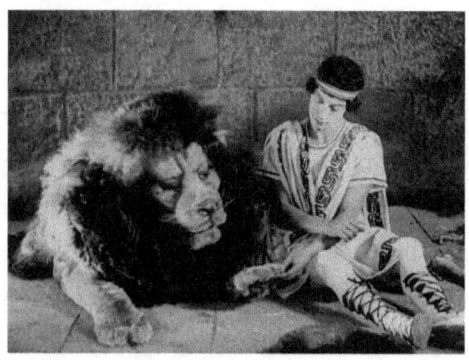 massively paid film star now, heading out into new territory. Three Ages is, in my view, the first true masterwork, though it doesn't measure to up to some of his snappier shorts, nor his finer full length achievements. It's an odyssey in three segments, each one covering different periods in time. Keaton made his first self-directed feature length movie this way just in case the film didn't quite work, so he could then at least divide it into three short movies. But work it did, and it proved to be a box office hit for him, even if some critics at the time didn't quite get what he was after.

The first segment of Three Ages concerns the prehistoric times, with Buster as a caveman. Despite the change of setting, it's very much the same old problem; Buster wants the girl but has a rival who is much bigger and more brutish than him. In the second story, Keaton is in Rome, again trying to win the affection of a rich girl. He partakes in some stunning stunts, including a chariot race, and gives himself plenty of opportunities to wow the audience. The final section has Keaton, once again, as a poor man looking for love with a rich man's daughter. At little over an hour, each 20 minute tale is just long enough to hold the interest, and while it may seem slightly like cheating to have your debut feature as three shorts put into one, it was also rather a clever decision, and ahead of its time. Using love and the yearning for riches as his thematic chord, the film works as a meditation on romance, and the class/wealth divide.

Some saw his idea of love through time, it being the central aim for all ages, as rather daft, and the film was met with criticism from some areas of the press. "Buster Keaton testifies that love goes unchangingly on through the years," wrote Photoplay, "and gives demonstrations in the stone age, the Roman era, and the present. There are some good moments, but as a whole the picture is dull and stolid. Margaret Leahy, the Talmadges' English importation, is as wooden as a chubby little blonde girl can be. And Wallace Beery is wasted as the comedy villain. No chance for uproarious laughter."

That Buster was no longer strictly going for "uproarious laughter" seemed to be lost on some reviewers at the time, but these days Keaton experts and film historians understand he was trying to broaden and expand the comedic film. As Terry Jones later said, "Keaton was the first time I realised comedy could be beautiful." And

Three Ages is certainly beautiful, a stunning film to look at and come back to time and time again.

Buster's second directed feature is Our Hospitality, another leap on from his previous work (at this point, Keaton somehow seems to mostly get better from picture to picture), With a script by Clyde Bruckman, Jean Havez and Joseph Mitchell, the film follows more of a cohesive plot than we had seen before in Buster's work, but the jokes came just as thick and fast, though they were most subtly applied to the pace and flow of the picture. A seven-reeler, it feels very much like the first full feature of his career, and more complete

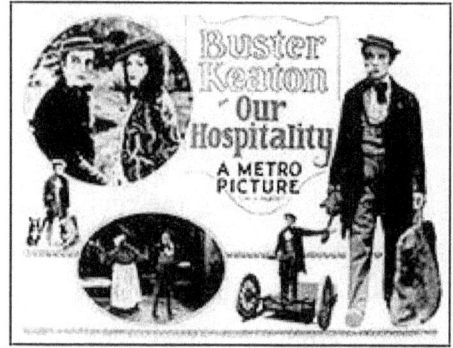

than both The Saphead and Three Ages.

The plot follows, like his earlier short Neighbors, the lives of two warring families, the Canfields and the McKays, a rivalry which ends up in the deaths of the heads of both households. After her husband is declared dead, the McKay wife moves away with her infant son to New York. Buster then grows up, but knows nothing of his father's bloody demise. He journeys to Scotland to retrieve his inheritance, where he meets a girl, then her father, Keaton regular Joe Roberts . (Sadly it turned out to be his last film role, as he died after filming.) Of course, as you might expect, the girl turns out to be a Canfield. Though Buster was raised not knowing of the feud, it seems inevitable that the McKays and the Canfields will forever be enemies.

44

It seems odd, at fist anyway, that Buster doesn't appear, as he had before in his shorts, within the first couple of minutes or so, but the opening sequence itself is truly stunning, one of the finest scenes, technically and aesthetically, of the early 1920s. When Keaton does appear however, it is very much worth the wait. Top hatted and something of a cloddish rich boy, within no time at all he has us rolling about; for instance, his bike scene is hilarious (where did these ideas come from?), and the travel sequence where Keaton and the girl make their way to the location is magnificent.

Though thick with gags as usual, there had been a drastic shift in Buster's approach to filmmaking. Yes he had had eyes on the ball throughout his proto shorts, but here, the framing is exquisite in each shot and Buster (along with co-director John Blystone) has somehow made every scene, every set up and every frame a work of art in itself. Though The General takes much of the credit (perhaps rightly so), I can see why some see Our Hospitality as his great masterpiece. Maybe Roger Ebert had a point...

Buster made changes in other ways too, not just visually. He ensured the story unravelled more dramatically and sustained a 74 minute (7 reel) viewing. Keaton got the idea from the real life Hatfield-McCoy feud, and as a life long train enthusiast he wanted to incorporate it into the story. Some of the finest scenes of Buster's career involved the train lines, and some of those are included in this remarkable film, which still looks and feels fabulous all these years on. For the first time, Keaton has totally captured another age, in this case the 1830s, with brilliant costumes and believable settings. In true Keeton style, he risked his life during filming, nearly drowning in the Truckee River where the picture was filmed. Thankfully for us he was OK, but was force to shoot the remainder of the scene on an LA set instead, clearly a little shook up by the incident. The film also features three Keatons, Buster's dad, Buster and Buster's baby son, the only film to contain the three generations together.

So Keaton was well under way, and Our Hospitality is evidence that he clearly knew where he was heading. The train obsession had come into place, and the weird desire to keep moving (Keaton is nearly always in motion of some sort, whether by foot or on a track) and there was only one way from here - up, for the time being at least.

Sherlock Jr. is for many a true masterpiece, a feature film with Buster at his best on all fronts; and I have to say, I wholeheartedly love the picture. Three Ages was good in its own way, but Sherlock Jr. exposed and projected the magic of cinema, the illusions it paints, and how one can get majestically swept up in its power. Keaton does so literally in the picture, and we as viewers, some ninety odd years down the line, do the same. This is surreal, playful and technically brilliant, with Keaton as the projectionist who walks right into the movie the punters are paying to see, and goes off on various adventures all of his own. Taking on the guise of a detective called Sherlock Jr., the film becomes a surreal film with a film, a head spinner even now; god knows how it must affected viewers back in 1924.

Photoplay loved it, writing, "Buster Keaton with a lot of new gags. He appears as a young man with a flair for amateur sleuthing. He has radical adventures. This is by no means Keaton's most hilarious offering, but it is short, snappy and amusing. Comedies are like oases in a celluloid world, rare and refreshing, and you don't want to miss

Buster with his immobile face and unique composure in his new setting."

Variety, however, just didn't get what Buster was up to, writing, "This Buster Keaton feature length comedy is about as unfunny as a hospital operating room. The picture has all the old hoke in the world in it. That ranges from a piece of business with a flypaper to a money-changing bit and, for added good measure, a chase. There are, in fact, two chases; but neither can for a single second hold a candle to Harold Lloyd. In comparison they appear child's play."

For his next picture, Keaton teamed up with director Donald Crisp, and co wrote a script with Clyde Bruckman, Jean Havez and Joseph

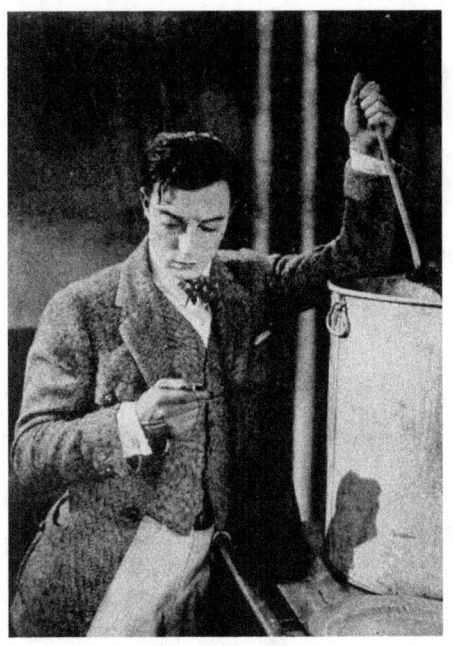 Mitchell which would result in the hit classic The Navigator. On a budget of 380,000 dollars, Buster was inspired by a visit to a 5,000 ton ship that was being scrapped off. Seeing as the boat was destined for destruction, Keaton and his crew decided to construct a tale employing the near endless possibilities of the vessel. Amazingly, Keaton and his gang reworked and remodelled the inside of the boat, and finished their movie in a 10 week shoot. However, Keaton did not get on that well with Crisp and ensured he was off the set for

half of the shoot, by pretending the shoot was over, and then carrying on when he had departed, without his input.

The water sequences were filmed later in a pool, then to Lake Tahoe when the scenes proved too complex. It went over budget, causing producer Schenck to lose his rag, but the film still doubled its costs at the box office. That was it, Keaton was not only an artist in his prime, accomplishing seemingly impossible feats on film, he was also making his studio a lot of money in the process.

In the picture, Keaton stars as Rollo, a young man who, after proposing to the woman across the road, Betsy (played by Kathryn McGuire), and getting a rejection, goes out on a solo cruise trip to Honolulu. Typically, as the boat number is obscured, he boards the wrong ship. It turns out that the rich father of Betsy has just sold it off to a small nation currently at war. Despite attempts to warn Buster/Rollo, Betsy ends up on the ship with him, and the pair attempt to adapt to their new life as seafarers. Rollo ends up in a diving suit to fix a hole on the ship, and Betsy is kidnapped by locals. At an hour long (six reels), the film flies by and remains one of Keaton's smoothest, tightest features.

As a stand alone film, The Navigator is often breath taking. Rather than laugh out loud funny, it's a picture, as a whole, to be slightly in awe of. Keaton too excels throughout, performing unbelievable stunts and skirting over the edge of what many would define as sane behaviour.

Keaton claimed The Navigator to be his finest film, and many might agree with him. It has an indescribable sense of magic about it, an artist at the top of his game and given freedom to do as he pleases. He would rarely get these chances again, so one can understand why

Keaton felt this was his finest work. The jokes are brilliant, slapstick with a twist at their best, and the visuals are fabulous. You wouldn't think he could top this, but of course - arguably, it has to be said, though there is a very good argument for it - he did.

Seven Chances may not be the most celebrated Keaton Golden era feature, but I have a soft spot for it. Something about the whole feel and pace make it a very warm and appealing picture. The gags are excellent, and the idea that Buster will inherit 7 million dollars if he is married by 7.00 pm that night is a touch of genius. Of course, what can go wrong does go wrong throughout, and the film goes from one frantic misunderstanding/chaotic predicament to another. It features, what are in my view, two of the best Keaton sequences from this era; the church scene where all the brides have turned up (some clearly men, many in make shift wedding outfits); and the hilarious and frankly quite astonishing avalanche scene, where a fleeing Keaton is chased down a hill by a sea of rocks, which then end up aiding him in getting rid of the pursuing, relentless brides with dollar signs in their eyes.

The inept hopeless young man in the danger zone of love was at it again. Like One Week, Buster is warning of the dangers of marriage, of an established life, but here, in the space of a speedy 56 minute six-reeler, he does so with continued hilarity. The fact it was a sole directorial piece for him also speaks a lot. After a frosty collaboration with Crisp on his last film, The Navigator, Buster was destined to go out alone and ensure he had 100 percent control. Though he did not write the screenplay (it was based on the Roi Cooper Megrue play), it was Keaton's perfect comic timing, his daring physicality and cinematic flair that made the story truly enthralling. Keaton had not been a fan of the play (he called it a sappy farce), but he had to make the film to settle a debt with Schenck, who had bought the rights to the play to be filmed. Funny then that it should result in one of his snappiest, tidiest pictures. It also proved to be a hit, the public clearly loving the chance to see Keaton in a desperate, restless farce such as this.

Reviews were mixed though, with some US critics dismissing it as sour. Again, the UK lapped it up, and Time Out wrote a smashing review: "Less ambitious and less concerned with plastic values than the best of Keaton, this is nevertheless a dazzlingly balletic comedy in which Buster has a matter of hours to acquire the wife on which a seven million dollar inheritance depends. From this leisurely start, the film takes off into a fantastically elaborate, gloriously inventive chase sequence, in which Buster escapes the mob of pursuing harridans only to find an escalating avalanche of rocks taking over at his heels as he hurtles downhill. Added only after an initial preview, the rocks make for one of the great Keaton action gags."

Keaton and Arbuckle had gone Out West a few years earlier, but Keaton's very different west-set comedy remains very much a stronger and more accomplished piece of filmmaking. Go West features Keaton as a chap named "Friendless", who heads west to get rich, ends up doing various jobs (bronco busting, cattle work, even a spot of farming) and becomes attached to a cow called Brown Eyes, who he tries to save from the slaughter house by using every and any means he can. Go West is one of Keaton's more soft and warm films, though in my view it doesn't come close to the films surrounding it in this era. Still, Friendless is a great character and there are some fabulous gags throughout. That said, it rarely elevates to the level of high art evident in other works.

The same can be said for Battling Butler, a minor Keaton picture where he stars as Alfred, sent by his dad on a fishing trip, where he falls for a mountain girl. Based on the stage play by Walter Rosemont and Ballard MacDonald, it feels less involved and inspired than films like The Navigator. But still, comparing it to such masterpieces is doing it an injustice, and any Keaton film in this era is a gem of some sort.

Anyone worried that Keaton's run of perfection had ended need not. The next film he directed is his mighty 1926 masterpiece, the monumental achievement that is The General. Inspired by the Great Locomotive Chase during the American Civil War, it was also lifted form the book by William Pittenger, all about his adventures on the railroad. Though The General was only a modest hit upon release, making a million back on a staggering - for the time - $750,000 budget, it also failed to impress the critics, who for some reason wrote the film off as inconsequential and unimportant. Now of course, it's beyond classic filmmaking. It's genius, up there with the finest cinematic works in history

Filmed in Oregan, where some old time railroads still existed, Keaton had found the ideal destination for his true masterpiece. Arriving in May of 26 with their mass amount of props, filming began in June. This was self-indulgence of the highest order, with Keaton at the steering wheel of one of the most lavish and expensive films of the era (filming cost $400 an hour apparently); clearly, he was in his element.

Comedy aside, and even though The General is genuinely funny, it is in the stunt and set piece departments where the film stuns the most. The destruction of the train, definitely the biggest scene in silent comedy history, remains frighteningly intense and, dare I say it, plain bonkers, and Keaton's dare devil stunts on the trains are unmatched to this day. No one in their right mind would attempt such feats today, and in Buster's era his daring was near supernatural.

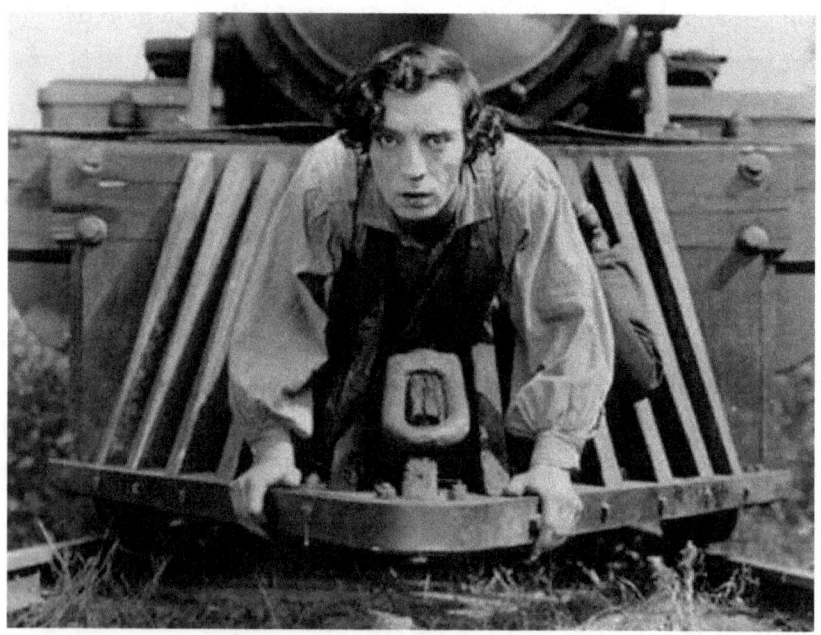

At the time though, these shenanigans went over the heads of most viewers, the people at the studio and, most of all, the press. Variety deemed it a flop and said it was far from funny. Research reveals that there are hardly any positive contemporary notices for The General. The rejection dinted Keaton's self confidence and sense of judgement. Though The Navigator was his favourite, he was also very keen on The General. "I was more proud of that picture than any

I ever made. Because I took an actual happening out of the history books, and I told the story in detail too."

The General sits in Keaton's filmography as Citizen Kane does in Orson Welles', a singular moment of genius that somehow, unexplainably so, turned out better than anyone could have imagined. All the elements were there, but the result was totally unexpected. Today, it's his classic.

The film's reputation started to change around the time Andrew Sarris wrote of Keaton and The General, in his book American Cinema: Directors and Directions. "The difference between Keaton and Chaplin," he states, "is the difference between prose and poetry, between the aristocrat and the tramp, between adaptability and dislocation, between the function of things and the meaning of things, eccentricity and mysticism, between man as a machine and man as angel, between girl as convention and girl as ideal. There are those who would go further and claim Keaton as pure cinema as opposed to Chaplin's essentially theatrical cinema."

Years on from Sarris's praise, younger film buffs and writers have elevated it further. In 2014, Sense of Cinema wrote a piece on the film, and used it to define Keaton's current standing alongside his silent comedy contemporaries. "Of the three great American clowns of the silent era, Charlie Chaplin, Buster Keaton and Harold Lloyd, Keaton has emerged, by and large, as the cinephiles' favourite over Chaplin, who was the greater star of his day and held the pre-eminent position in critics' eyes for the first half of the last century. Although both Chaplin and Keaton were remarkably gifted physical performers, Keaton's gags rely on a combination of his amazing physical abilities with the apparatus of the cinema – editing, pacing and camera placement. The General, which he considered his favourite, was Keaton's last independently produced film and in many ways presents the apotheosis of his style."

TCM recently summed it up nicely, writing, "When the Museum of Modern Art in New York scheduled a tribute to United Artists in 1955, The General was the only film so in demand it had to be shown twice. It was voted one of the ten best films ever made in British film magazine Sight and Sound's international critics survey in 1972 and again in 1982. In 1989, it was one of the first films to be voted onto the National Film Registry, marking its official recognition as a national treasure."

Following up The General won't have felt intimidating at the time for Buster, because the film was so cruelly dismissed anyway. Only in hindsight does his next film seem so pale in comparison, even though it has its own set of charms. College, released in 1927, runs at little over an hour, and concerns Buster as Ronald, a high school graduate who longs to win the heart of Mary (Anne Cornwall), and tries to woo her with his inept sports skills, obviously to no avail. Mary becomes charmed by his clumsy attempts to win her over and despite his flaws, falls for him. The only problem left is the matter of Jeff (Harold Goodwin), Mary's "jock" boyfriend. However, when Ronald and Mary team together (basically by throwing stuff at him), they reign victorious, get married, and, though it's a cliché, live happily ever after.

There is always a tidy simplicity to many of Keaton's films in this period, a fairytale, child like quality where the good guy gets the girl, and the bad guy gets zilch. Marriage and children spell eternal joy in Buster's world, even if the conquest of love is often riddled with mini horror stories. In the end, Buster's efforts are worth the trouble, and true love is good for the soul.

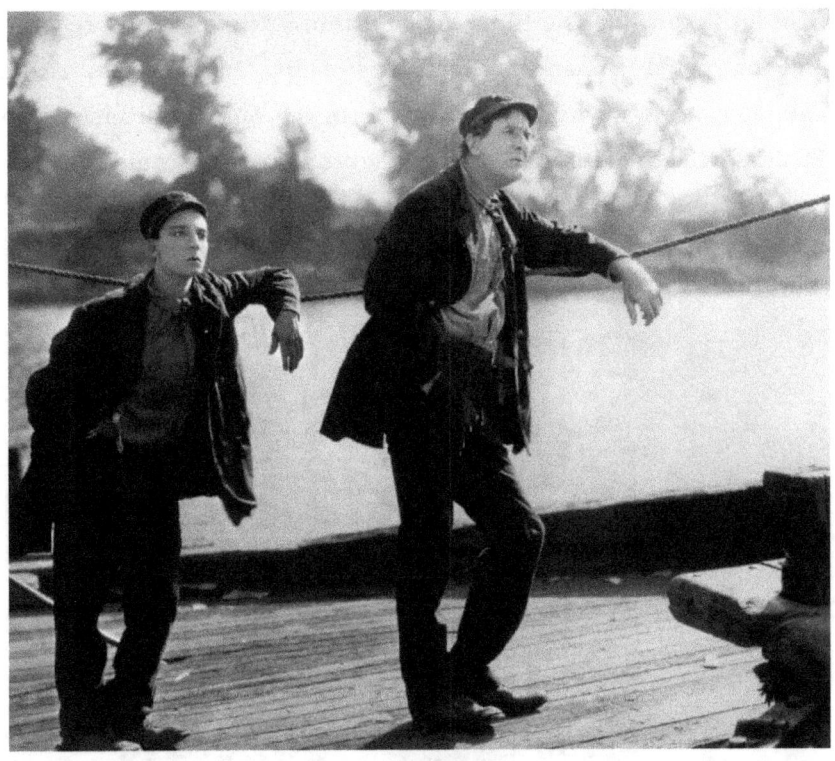

Steamboat Bill Jr. marked the end of an era for Buster, in that it was the last film he released with his own production team, before signing over to MGM, a decision he later lived to regret. But Steamboat Bill Jr. remains classic Keaton, the story of a steamer captain (played by Ernest Torrene) awaiting the arrival of his son, who is a college student - this is Buster where Buster comes in. He has not seen Jr. since he was a boy, and expecting a rugged, strapping lad, he is surprised to be met by the diminutive Buster.

Keaton comes across as some kind of proto-Woody Allen here, a shuffling, awkward, nervy young man who clearly disappoints his old man on first sight. The film winds off into a tale of family rivalries and unwanted romances (Keaton is dating his business rival's daughter, always a trigger for trouble in the Buster universe), with Buster forced to become the hero he never thought he could be.

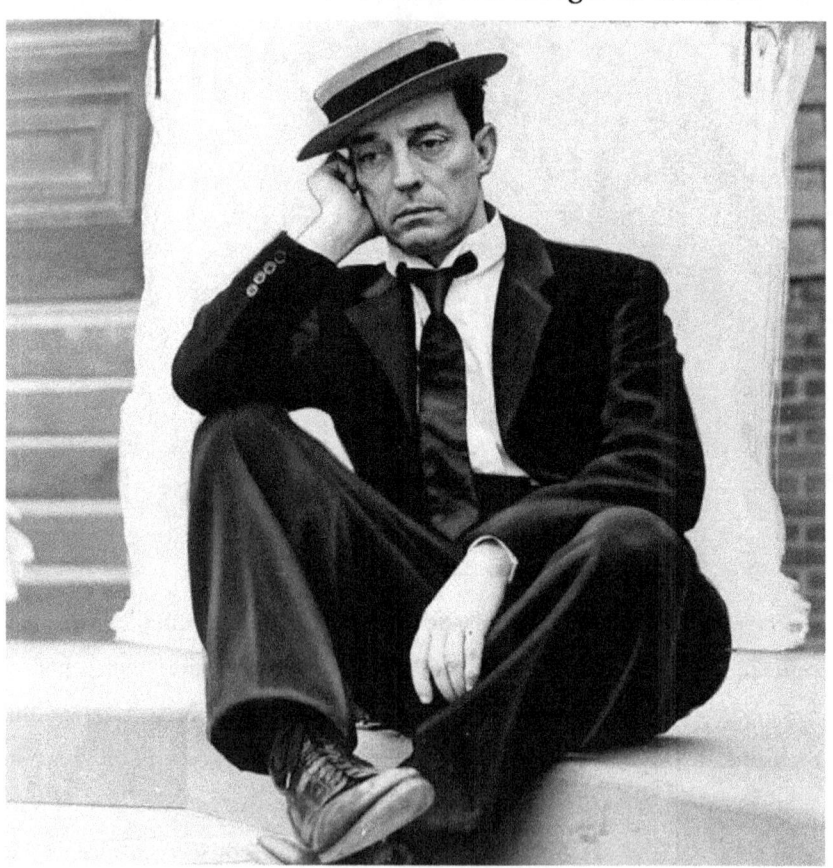

This was the back end of the free era when Buster's creativity could run riot, and perhaps he knew so, hence why he went out to Sacramento and spent $100,000 on sets. Maybe he figured, 'if I'm gonna lose my control, I'd better lose it in style.' The budget ran up to hundreds of thousands (a fortune in the day), but the results, one might argue, were worth the trouble. The movie is an immortal classic, and will be remembered for the classic "window frame" scene when the house falls on him, but he is saved by the window frame. He had made a masterpiece, but it didn't matter one jot. By the end of production, it was announced by Schenck that Buster Keaton Productions was no more. Buster was reckless, disappointed and bitter, risking his life on a stunt that he knew could easily have killed him. Had he not felt rock bottom, he claimed he would never have performed such a ludicrous stunt. "I was mad at the time," he later remarked, "or I would never have done the thing."

Steamboat Bill Jr. was a flop at the box office, and reviews were poor too. Keaton had fallen from grace as quickly as he had risen to fame and fortune. His personal life began to unravel and though he made one more picture in this style, the excellent, dazzling The Cameraman, it was the end of the line in regards to his wild, artistically liberated era. Signed up with MGM, he called it the biggest mistake of his career. Ironically, of course, the Cameraman was a box office hit, making three quarters of a million at the box office. Still, the damage was done and Keaton's pride had been severely dinted. He hated the way MGM worked, said there were too many people around interfering with his choices, and he was just another star on a roster.

He saw the twenties out with Spite Marriage, a neat Keaton comedy (an 80 minuter no less) made in collaboration with Edward Sedgwick for MGM. Buster plays Elmer Gantry, a dry cleaner who worships Trilby Drew (Dorothy Sebastian), a film idol more interested in fellow actor Lionel (Edward Earle). After a series of mishaps and farcical happenings, Elmer and Trilby find themselves reconnecting, in true classic Keaton style.

Spite Marriage was OK, with some clever gags and nice performances, but Keaton wanted to make it as a sound film. MGM refused flat out, saying their primitive sound recording equipment was reserved mostly for musicals. It was a bullshit excuse. MGM were simply not willing to play. Buster was to go on and make talkies in the next couple of years, but the magic had dimmed, the fire had gone out a little in his eyes, and he couldn't help but regret not taking Chaplin's advice and turning down MGM flat.

Finishing off his glory decade with one of his weaker efforts, Keaton would find that the 1930s were not to be so kind to him, though he did do some good work in this era. In 1932, the studio came up with the strange idea of pairing him with Jimmy Durante, with whom he made a string of talkie comedies, The Passionate Plumber, Speak Easily and What! No Beer? They were popular movies in their day, but Buster was not entirely satisfied to say the least. They have not aged so well, and Keaton and Durante's styles jar horridly.

By 1932/33, Keaton was down and out. Tired from having to shoot each of his new sound films multiple times in different languages, and saddened by his loss of creative freedom, Keaton was drinking so heavily it was affecting his work. He hated the openly mocking What! No Beer? and is clearly drunk during some scenes in the finished cut. After the filming was completed, MGM bluntly fired him, coldly sending out a letter that said his services were no longer required. At the same time, his marriage to Talmadge came to an end, with her having enough of his drinking and affairs. His drinking worsened still, as did his mental state, to the point that he thought that rats and insects were attacking him. For a brief spell he was even put in a strait jacket and forced to give up the booze. It was a sad come down for the genius of silent comedy.

After some trips abroad for low budget comedies, Keaton signed up for a 16 picture deal (making two-reelers) with Educational Pictures, a real step backwards. These quickies were among the best work he did in the wilderness of his post-glory years, through the 30s and 40s, and any Keaton fan will delight in their quickfire gaggery. This brief phase of light was not to last though, and when the series of shorties ended, Keaton was re-employed by MGM on a wage of $100 a week, writing gags for the Marx Brothers, none of which they seem to have used. It was a hiring done out of pity more than anything, and he received no credit for any of this work.

At the end of the 1930s, with a botched second marriage behind him that he rarely liked to discuss, Keaton signed up with Columbia for a ten film deal, a series of two-reeler comedies. Buster found himself begging for them to let him direct a single short. Keaton looked back upon the Columbia years as the worst on an artistic level. By the time he got to the last two-reeler, She's Oil Mine, Keaton declared he would never again find himself making "another crummy two reeler."

The forties were a rather strange time on a professional level for Buster, with many forgettable roles in obscurities not really worthy of his name. But he needed the money, so he kept on working in whatever he could. On the plus side, he met Eleanor, with whom he enjoyed a healthy, happy marriage until his dying day.

Not much of Keaton's work in the 1940s has lasted or endured that well, but he was working towards a comeback that was both unlikely and unconventional. At the back end of the forties, Life Magazine published a piece on Buster that seemed to sum up his status in that era. "Perhaps because dry comedy is so much more rare and odd than dry wit," James Agee said, "there are people who never much cared for Keaton. Those who do cannot care mildly."

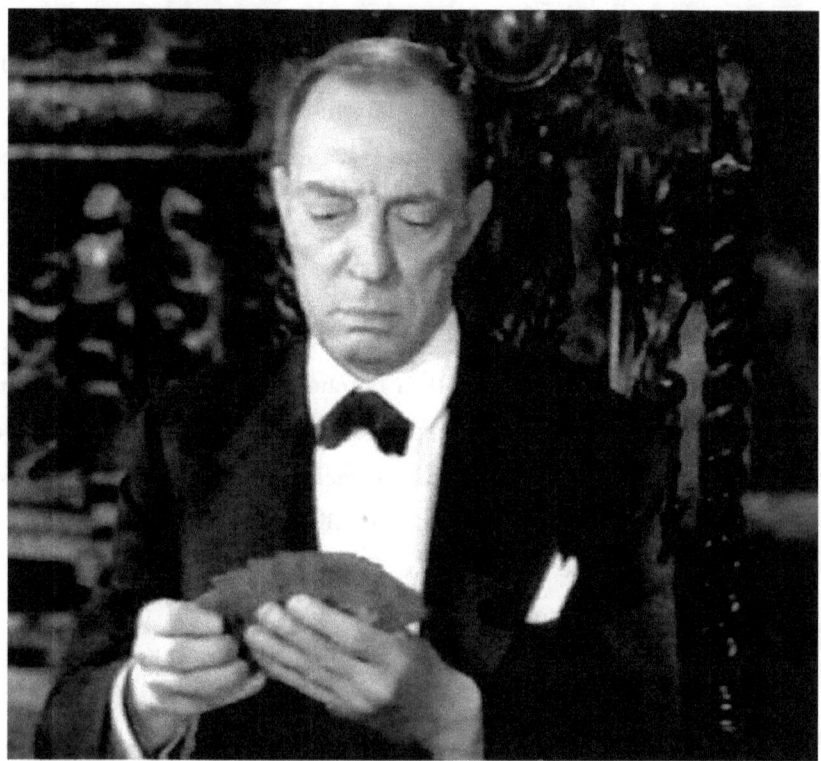

The feeling in the air was that he belonged in a bygone age, and Hollywood didn't have enough room for such an old fashioned star. This relic was confined to crackly old silent comedies, the quality of which was deteriorating as the decades went on. As if to tidily and bluntly put this theory to celluloid, Buster was cast in a small role in the 1950 Hollywood classic Sunset Boulevard, one of the finest mainstream films of the era. The only problem here was that Buster's cameo was not an entirely glamorous one; in fact it was demeaning. He is one of the old faded film stars, referred to as the Waxworks, who plays bridge with Gloria Swanson's Norma Desmond, herself a has-been from the silent era. Buster and his crusty card playing buddies were living, breathing metaphors for a rotten, cruel Hollywood, and were given little time or room to do anything else but stand for the countless old timers chewed and spat out by the system. Still, even in such a small scene, there was no denying how Keaton's face burst from the screen, an immortal collection of features saying in one word and one expression what the director (Billy Wilder) spent the whole film doing. Despite the subtle strength of his cameo, in retrospect it seems sad and degrading to have him referred to as a mere waxwork. Still, it's a brilliant scene, and is evident that Keaton was willing to swallow his pride for the sake of a good scene, and of course a nice pay cheque. Sunset Boulevard reflected the pathetic, depressing side of Hollywood, and exposed stardom as an empty illusion. Buster knew it more than anyone.

In many ways, though rather tragic, the scene began a turnaround in Keaton's life and career, though not directly. Agee's essay, written twenty years after his glory years, was penned in the midst of Buster's lost, hopeless phase. But a change was just around the corner. Within twelve months, Agee's story might have read much differently. Rather than talking about Keaton in a past tense as if deceased, he would be waxing lyrical about his latest comedy adventures. And though Agee is right in saying that "Keaton played mostly for laughs", the depth of his performances only grew more involving, effective and affecting in the next few years, the journeyman comic who'd come out the other end with a story to tell and a face to prove it.

LIMELIGHT

When Two Silent Legends Shared the Screen

"The audience thinks that we think in different channels. We automatically think in the same channel, but my way of doing it and Chaplin's way are two different ways. I've always been friendly with Chaplin socially. We spoke the same language. I've changed gags with Chaplin – given him gags that didn't fit me."

- Buster Keaton on Chaplin

Just as Keaton was on the rise as a star of television in the early 1950s, he got a call from an old friend and rival, the legendary Charlie Chaplin. Thirty odd years earlier the two men had been the guiding lights in silent film comedy, with Harold Lloyd close behind, each one coming up with killer film after killer film. Chaplin could unveil masterpieces like The Gold Rush and City Lights, but Keaton had The Navigator, The General and Seven Chances to his name. Chaplin had sweetness, sentimentality and loveability, Keaton had realness, invention, mechanical genius and an honesty that was harsher than Chaplin's Tramp persona. Comparing Keaton and Chaplin is a messy affair though, and one can fall into the all too familiar clichés if you're not careful. Yes, Chaplin used sentimentality to get the audience on his side, but he did so with such beauty that it instantly shoots down the naysayers who use it as a weapon against him. On the other hand, Keaton used his almost unearthly physical skills, his acrobatic abilities, to wow the viewer, but rarely, if ever, did he try to make you like him, nevermind feel sorry for him. Keaton left that open; you either cared or not. Of course, some people turn around and say that Buster's comedy is more cold, more one dimensional due to this fact, but I personally disagree. Admittedly, Chaplin was more accessibly appealing, but the mechanics of Keaton's work were much more complex and harder to fathom, thus more impressive. One could go on all day about the pros and cons of choosing one or the other, if you really wanted to waste time doing so, but the truth is both men were geniuses of their age, and had elements the other didn't, and perhaps wished they had.

Famously, Orson Welles was always pro-Keaton, and in his conversations with filmmaker Henry Jaglom (documented in the terrific book, My Lunches With Orson) in the 70s and 80s, he waxes lyrical of Buster to a degree that almost does a disservice to Chaplin. Welles had good reason to judge Chaplin though, after a less than satisfactory collaboration, but he sincerely felt Keaton was the superior comic, actor and director. He even claimed The General to be the best comedy of all time, perhaps the best film of all time, full stop. The man who made Citizen Kane, often called the best film ever made, and then spent 40 odd years trying to match its towering status, repeatedly called a has been and spent force, surely saw eye to eye with Keaton, the ageing legend who in the fifties saw a resurgence in his classic work, even though studios still wouldn't give him his own movie. Welles spent years trying to raise funds for his films, but the same people who put his early work on a pedestal (the movie brats of the 70s and 80s, and the studios who revered him) were not willing to put up the money. Keaton and Welles had a lot in common. "Now Keaton is coming in, I have no one to argue with anymore," Welles said in the seventies as Keaton's reputation soared. "I have always been saying, No, it's Keaton!"

Chaplin on the other hand, was a legend in his own time, a symbol of the universal appeal of good humour, and an icon matched by few, if any, figures of the early part of the 20th century. While Keaton's star declined in the thirties and forties, and his personal life became messier (he was drinking too heavily, his divorce was messy and, lest we forget, he was locked up for a short spell and put in a strait jacket), Chaplin's career rose still, so did his reputation as a genius. Buster was popping up in terrible films unworthy of his talent even back in the 1930s and early 40s, and Chaplin was still making some of his best pictures, like Modern Times and The Great Dictator. Keaton may have out classed Chaplin in the twenties, and been much more prolific too (Keaton recalled in one interview how lazy Chaplin was getting, declining to do two films a year as Buster had, and being content on making one a year, then one every two years, then one every three, and so on), Chaplin's status lasted longer. Into the early fifties, Buster was at least working, but some saw his TV roles as a sad come down, Chaplin included. It was in this period, with Chaplin in his early sixties and Keaton in his mid fifties, that the two men met once again, this time not as friends off screen, but as co stars on the big screen.

Limelight was one of Chaplin's finest latter day pieces. Made in 1952, it was a warm and knowing tragicomic tale set in the fickle and brittle world of live comedy. It fearlessly explored the pitfalls of being washed up, but intent on carrying on because, quite simply, you don't know how to do anything else. Written, directed, produced by and starring Chaplin, the film proved he had longevity, and that his skill went far beyond the crackly days of silent cinema. Chaplin was still relevant, and the world agreed.

In the film, Chaplin starred as a washed up comic who saves a girl from committing suicide. Shot for 900,000, it made back 7 million at the box office, and received rave notices. Today, it's considered one of his best films, and it's clear to see why. Less flat and broad than his earlier classics, the film had a sadness and a depth that was not only human, but also very moving on a more complex level. Chaplin had made yet another masterpiece, no question, and no one could accuse of it of being schmaltzy. The tragedy here was visceral.

The fact that Charlie wanted Keaton in his film is rather telling. Who else but an old rival from the roaring twenties would understand the conflicting sadness and glory of the comedian's existence? Keaton knew all too well the good and bad sides of show business, how you can be on top of the world one day and the bottom of the heap the next. But what made the "reunion" all the more sweet was the fact that Keaton was playing an old comedy partner, whose name we do not learn, with whom he performs a triumphant routine at a benefit gig. The final twist is the fact that Chaplin's Calvero has a heart attack, and dies at the side of the stage while watching another act. This was to be a comeback, but it ended up his swan song. Keaton is there for this ironic, tragic and ultimately devastating finale.

The idea of pairing Keaton and Chaplin is genius in itself, but what of their scenes together? In short they are magical. The two men, veterans in reality and within the film, look like they know a thing or two and have been round the block a few times, but there is a sweetness to their interaction. Seated before mirrors in the "star" dressing room, Keaton and Chaplin enjoy a marvellous moment applying their make up. Chaplin is confident and happy to be back in the spotlight, while Keaton provides the hilarious cynicism of a faded star. "If anyone else says it's like old times," he grumbles, "I'll jump out the window." The great thing is, of course, that we totally buy it. Unfortunately the scene is just too brief.

Thankfully, the stage performance is longer, and a wonder. Keaton, clad in a suit with mad scientist hair and a fake moustache, is at the piano and Chaplin standing with a violin. Chaplin's loose, Tramp-eque physicality is undimmed by the passing decades, and Keaton's bumbling is fantastic. By the end of the routine, one cannot help but regret they never worked on screen together again, or before this for that matter. But we all know Keaton and Chaplin were too big in their heyday, too iconic and egocentric, too famous and stubborn, to ever share the screen. Here, ageing and more modest, the two legends charm their way into the canon of classic comedy. What is also interesting to note is how each man sticks to their persona, at least in their delivery. Keaton remains stony faced, almost totally emotionless save for a feigned tearful episode after one of Chaplin's moving violin solos, and Chaplin pulls every face imaginable. In one brief moment, they remind the world what had made them the best at their respective, and very different, crafts.

The back-story to the pairing is almost as interesting as their on screen chemistry. Chaplin did not intend for Keaton to play the role at first, for he felt the part too small for such a star. However, when he learned of Buster's personal difficulties he wanted to help an old comrade. The contrast between Chaplin and Keaton's statuses in the early 1950s could not have been harsher. Chaplin owned his own studio, and was as much an icon as ever before. Limelight was even shot in Hollywood at his lot. Keaton, a man who once owned his own production company, had said goodbye to his home, family, fortune and bankability, a man who had had it all and lost it, now slowly clawing back some credibility, aided by a loyal wife. Keaton showed he was a big man though, taking such a small role in a movie by an ex rival whose career had sky rocketed while his had plummeted. But Keaton was an old pro, and he was way above pettiness and jealousy. Thankfully, he took the role.

There was no bad blood between the two men at all. Keaton waxed lyrical of Chaplin time and time again, and even mentioned him favourably in his memoir. Chaplin however, did not mention him in his own autobiography. He seems to have felt threatened by Keaton; not the man, but the artist, or rather the clown that he refused to accept as an artist on his own level. In the sixties and seventies, after Keaton's death, Buster's reputation started to catch up and perhaps even overtake Chaplin's. Charlie remained the biggest icon, recognisable in every country all over the world (the hat and 'tache did that effortlessly) but critics were beginning to see more worth in Buster's work. In his old age, Charlie enjoyed a fruitful retirement, but was alive to see the minor backlash against his work, the unfair claims of schmaltziness and audience manipulation. Keaton's work was only growing in acclaim and reverence in his absence.

Chaplin's daughter Geraldine once told a story about her dad which, in retrospect, is rather sad, seeing as he was undeniably one of the most famous icons in history. "I remember once, he was then very old," Gerladine said, "and I came with a boyfriend of mine, very interested in cinema. Not so interested in Chaplin. He preferred Buster Keaton, which was not the thing to do. We arrived, and he

68

spoke with my father a bit about silent films. And then he went on to talk about Buster Keaton, and my father just got smaller and smaller and he shrunk, and he was so hurt. It was like someone had stabbed him. And he just became very, very quiet. He didn't say a word during dinner. And after dinner he was thinking and he was looking into the fire, and suddenly he peeped in a little voice. He looked at my friend in the eye and he said: 'But I was an artist.' And no one knew what he was talking about. And then he said: 'You know, I gave him work.'"

Retrospectively, people see Keaton's brief role as a highlight of Limelight, and critics at the time were impressed too. Life Magazine raved about Keaton's work in the film, and reported the on set antics of the two geniuses, who would never appear on screen together again: "The scene with Buster Keaton, himself a star of the silent comedies, began with only the meager idea of a nearsighted pianist and an acrobatic violinist. The two, who had never appeared together before, spent a day of preparation in shirtsleeves organizing the piece of business which would form their act. With utter disregard of their ages (Keaton, 56, Chaplin, 63), they danced and tumbled, experimented, repeated. Stagehands, dancers, musicians sat in bemused groups breaking into laughter, applauding as they watched a show no one else would ever see"

Upstaged by Keaton or not, Chaplin need not have worried. His reputation was immovable, and even if some people did prefer Keaton to him, it seems rather sad that he should care. Keaton's idea of their rivalry was light, and despite Chaplin's popularity eclipsing his, Buster took it with pride, and honourably soldiered on.

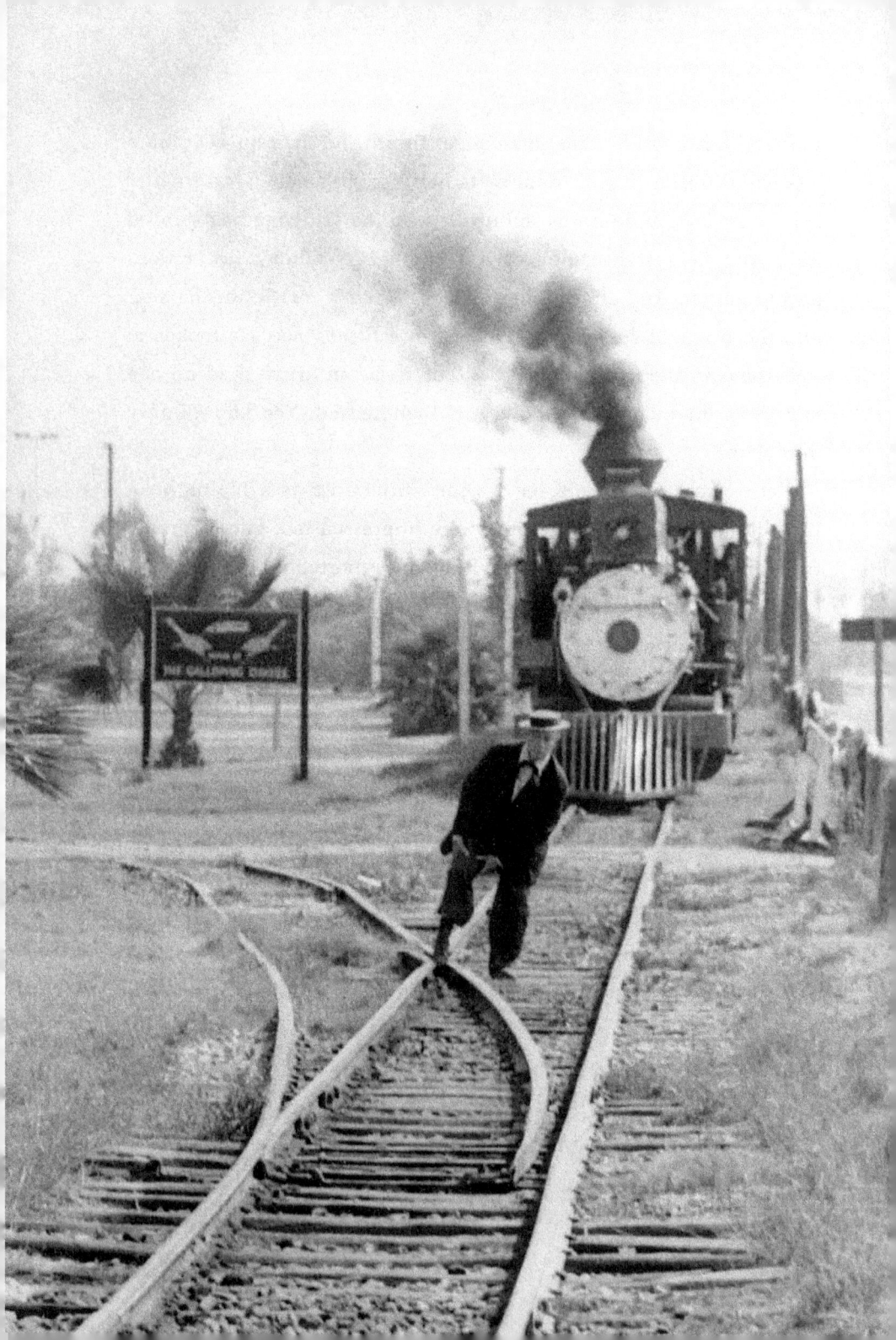

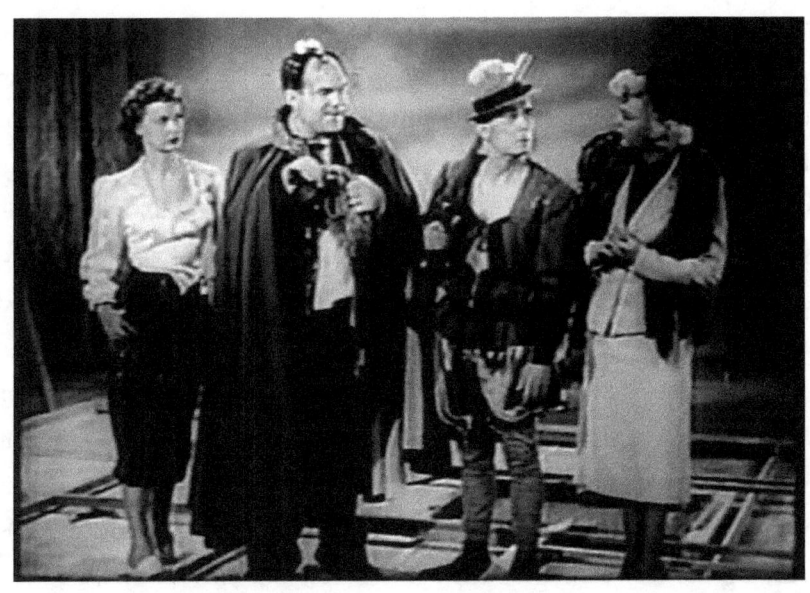

THE BUSTER KEATON SHOW

A Short Lived Small Screen Success

"By then I had almost given up hope of getting another real chance as an actor. I emphasize the word almost, because no one with actor's blood in his veins ever really admits to himself he is through, no matter what he says to other people..."

- Buster Keaton

Just as Keaton's cinematic reputation started to experience an upturn, almost perfectly at the start of a fresh new decade, the 1950s, the medium of television welcomed Buster with open arms. For many actors and performers, TV was something of a comedown, especially in regards to film, while others mistrusted this "new" medium, preferring the free, limitless, sonic wonders of radio. On radio, one could achieve anything, and if the production was to use sound effects, dialogue and music to their full capabilities, bring almost any story to life on air. Orson Welles proved this in the 1930s when his War of the Worlds was so believable that many Americans listening in their homes deemed the earth doomed, and went into a frenzied panic.

By the time Keaton appeared on the small screen, his film career was all but over. While many men would have been ashamed of going from the glamorous film lot to the creaky TV set, for Buster it was a saving grace. This silent comedy superstar had spent the 1930s drinking his way through rotten film roles, and an even more rotten marriage. The forties had been marginally better, but only slightly, with Keaton showing few signs of his genius in various forgettable, and indeed forgotten pictures. But television was perfect for a comic like Keaton. He could come on, do what he did best, and have the studio audience, and the viewers at home, in a fit of giggles. Running parallel to his cameo in Sunset Boulevard in 1950, he was given his own TV show, which proved to be a hit.

The Buster Keaton show went out on the Los Angeles channel KTTV, a small affiliate of CBS. Buster also made a one off the previous year, the TV special The Buster Keaton Comedy Show, but unfortunately the tapes do not exist. However, some episodes of The Buster Keaton Show can be enjoyed in all their glory.

Keaton got a glimpse into how other old time comedy veterans viewed TV. Buster recalled running into Chaplin in 1951, when he had offered him the part in Limelight. "He seemed astonished by my appearance," Keaton recalled. Apparently, after the horror stories of Keaton's drinking and his brief incarceration at a mental facility, Charlie was expecting a wreck. Chaplin asked his one time rival how he kept himself in such good shape. Keaton's reply? "Television..." Apparently, Chaplin gasped and turned a funny colour. "The subject of TV was never raised again," recalled Buster. This anecdote tells you how low TV was on the showbiz ladder back in the day, and how a vaudevillian veteran turned screen idol like Chaplin viewed it as a dirty word. And to be fair, you can see his point. To Chaplin, and Keaton too, comedy was epic. It wasn't just cheap laughs and a barrage of gags flying in your face, it was about subtlety, beauty and timing. The big screen was the perfect place for Chaplin and Keaton's brand of comedy, where it was taken seriously as an art form. Magical illusions could be achieved by using careful camera work and trickery. Cinema was magical, and so was their comedy. Taken off the big screen though, in Chaplin's view, the comedy lost much of its wonder, and once reduced to the cheap level of TV, was nothing more than a string of gags, funny but empty. Hearing that Buster was making his money on the small screen must have been a big shock to Chaplin, given the two men were head to head back in the 1920s, competing with each other with films like The Kid and The General. Indeed, it looked like a comedown, but for Buster, it was a comeback, and this game was about survival, focusing on the work, whatever form that work took on.

Buster wasn't going to get snooty about TV. After all, in his words, "TV had brought me back as an actor. By 1949, except for an occasional day's work, I had not put on grease paint for the cameras in almost five years. The summer theatres had put in no bids for my services since 1941. My most important engagement had been a four week date as a star of a famous Paris circus, back in 1947. So it was one of the thrills of my life when I got the chance in December of 1949 to do my own weekly TV show."

Buster later recalled: "The Buster Keaton Show was a success, but only on the West Coast where it gradually worked its way up to the position of Number One Comedy Program. In those days the only

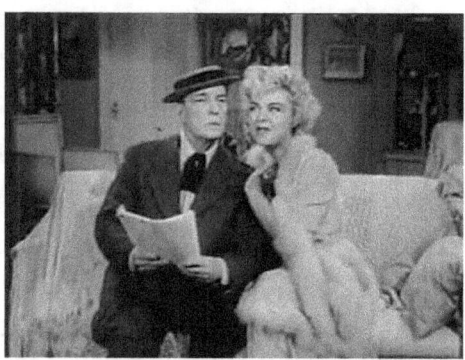

way to sell a Hollywood show to a national network was with kinetoscopes, and these were dismal things to look at eight or nine years ago. And my show was never sold to a sponsor as a coast-to-coast attraction. I think the story would have been different if I had waited for just two more years. But I had never, of course, wanted less to wait for anything. The important thing, though, was how these appearances on local television shows steamed up the interest of producers in other fields. I did about twenty-three Buster Keaton TV shows in 1950 and seventeen more in 1951. The same day I turned in the final 1951 show, Eleanor and I left for Paris to play a return engagement at the Paris circus. The date was so successful that I was booked for another four-week engagement during the following year."

Watching The Buster Keaton Show today, despite the ropey reputation among some admirers, the Keaton fan feels spoilt rotten with gem after gem. You can tell Keaton is relishing the chance to shine before a camera again, and be in control of the low budget, no frills gaggery. As he later said, he quit movies because there were too many cooks in the kitchen, and "on TV I can go back to creating my own show. Only three of us are working on it." So for Buster, it was a case of simplifying matters. And The Buster Keaton Show is certainly that, stripped down to the basics of what made Buster so great.

It seems funny today that The Studebakers start each episode off with an endorsement of their cars, but this is how it was done in the early days of TV; no high production adverts, just a straight forward plug of a product, followed by "Now, it's time for the Buster Keaton show..." One of the surviving episodes of the show is the great boxing fight, the "getting you in shape" scenario, where Keaton plays an aging fighter, clearly in shape already, getting sorted out by a trainer in a gymnasium for the big fight. Keaton is in his mid 50s at this point, but his agility and flexibility is truly remarkable.

Though these sketches are a little cornier and more dated than some of his golden big screen gems (it's mostly down to the other actors though, not Keaton, who is fabulous throughout), you cannot deny how funny they are. Buster, looking diminutive, excels at the rope skip ("I used to be good at this..."), ends up wrestling with a dummy in the corner of the hall, and shoots some hoops in classic Keaton fashion. Though he interacts beautifully with the other performers (and if truth be told, makes them all a little better), his solo scenes are close to being magical, despite the flat camerawork and grainy quality. Shot with one camera mostly from a distance, dust this off and it's Buster gold. The laughter gives it that old American TV vibe, but otherwise there is not much here to make it differ too drastically from his old films. Buster is in great shape for his age too, and one can see why Chaplin made a reference to it.

When it comes down to the fight, Buster is hilarious, possibly the worst boxer in history, stumbling and blocking clumsily like a lost boy. He takes a couple right in the chops too and falls down majestically. In the end, however, he is victorious. The crowd go nuts.

While many saw this as a come down, Buster must have felt like he'd had a good day at the office. And even though only LA dwellers saw it at the time, the shows have gained a cult following down the years, thanks in part to the internet and its endless wonders.

The episodes went down so well in fact that they decided to make a version that could go out across the country, titled Life With Buster. This was not as well received however, but today the shows look just as good as the smaller KTTV broadcasts. Thankfully it survives to this day, an hour long collection that is full of mini moments of Buster magic and joy.

Things got better still, proving that the TV show had been a good decision. In 1951, they assembled a film of the show's finest sketches, The Misadventures of Buster Keaton, which went over to the UK, where Keaton's star still shone brightly. The film did well and still to this day hangs together successfully. So while his old rivals may have frowned upon the idea of such a giant as Keaton "reducing" himself to TV, and though the results were often a little creaky and painfully low budget, Keaton could get gold out of the medium, and come out looking respectful with dignity intact.

Buster as a TV star seems to make a lot of sense, but imagining his contemporaries having weeklies on the small screen seems odd somehow. Yes, Groucho Marx had become a staple on the box, but he was something of an exception, and a man always known for his quick wit and savage put downs was ideal for the game show and panel circuit. The idea of him doing a sketch show though seems rum. The same goes for Chaplin. At this point he was retired, film royalty residing in his throne. And when he did come out in the sixties, it was to direct features, which rarely matched his classics - Countess From Hong Kong being a prime example. That said, it seems impossible to imagine Chaplin, the legendary tramp, treading the boards of TV. It comes down to ego, maybe a bit of pride too, and the fact that Chaplin's wealth and continued control over his own work meant that he didn't have to do anything he didn't truly wish to.

Indeed, on the other end of things, the main reason Buster could swallow his pride and appear on TV, bringing his bumbling persona to millions of viewers, was due to what many people have often called his lack of ego. He knew he'd had it all at one point, and the reasons he had lost it was largely his own fault; the drinking, going over budget, refusing to play the Hollywood game etc. It was self inflicted, though it's arguable if Keaton could have avoided it. But Chaplin was a god, an Englishman who had risen from nothing (literally, he was once homeless for a short spell), became a star of the English stage, conquered Hollywood, and redefined comedy by making it sad and beautiful.

Buster on the other hand was living modestly, working hard and living from week to week. He was still out there hustling, and TV had an excitement about it. "TV meant the live audience," he once said with enthusiasm. The great thing about it was that Eleanor was now his true equal, and delighted audiences when she appeared on the small screen alongside her husband in their hilarious double act. "I was just one more prop to be dumped on my head," she said with a smile, "just like his other leading ladies."

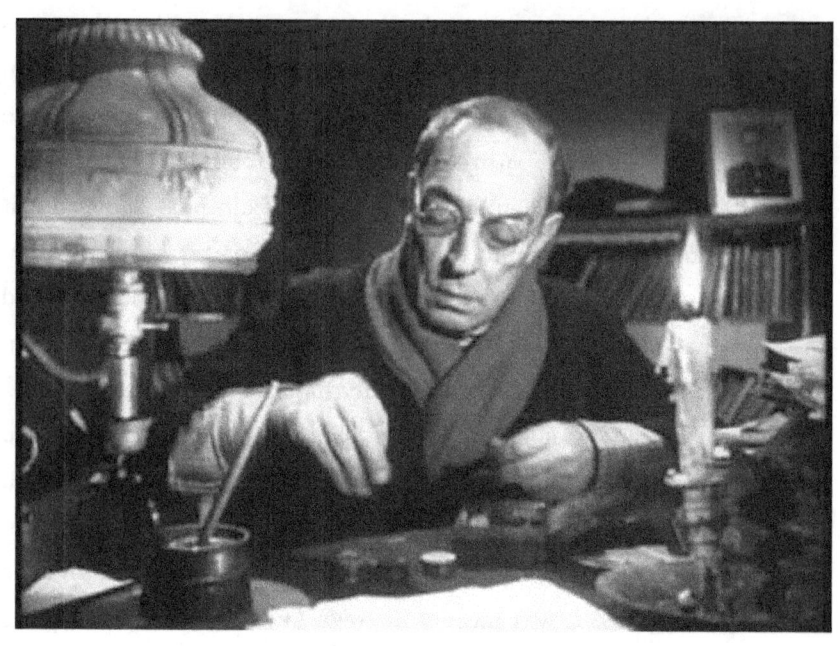

THE AWAKENING

Buster Keaton Gets Serious As the Man

Working outside his comfort zone, Keaton found himself being cast in more out-there productions on the small screen. In 1954 Buster appeared in an episode of Douglas Fairbanks Jr. Presents, called The Awakening. It was remarkable for a few reasons. For one, Buster played it straight, and the results were truly fabulous. Called simply The Man in this wonderfully shot TV film, Buster takes centre stage in an update of Nikolai Gogol's story and delivers a fantastic performance. I think it's one of his finest efforts, a man showing his natural talent as an actor and using his charisma to get by, without the aid of falls and gags. It was another edge to the Keaton prism.

As the bureaucrat who rebels against the strict regime of the machine (we are in Orwellian 1984-esque territory here), Buster's part was rumoured to be a reference to the red fears of the 1950s, and The Awakeneing was being whispered about as an anti communism piece of propaganda disguising itself as entertainment. Though you might be excused for labelling it a Better Red Than Dead piece of metaphorical mind control, that's just too lazy a conclusion to come to. Besides, Fairbanks Jr. was adamant it was not the case. "Our story is anywhere or nowhere," he enigmatically explained. "The time; yesterday, today or in the tomorrows to come."

The story itself, with Keaton being in charge of a sizeable database listing all the notable and minute details about people's lives, seems more relevant today than ever before, especially in regards to Facebook, social media and the control the digital medium has on us all. Fairbanks, in his introduction, says it's a film about a man who forgets the true meaning of freedom, and is willing to sacrifice himself on the altar. For American TV, it was deep stuff.

The plot moves on when Keaton goes to a tailor and asks him to fix up a coat. But the tailor deems it unfixable. "What am I, a tailor or a magician?" asks the tailor, pointing to the rubbish people bring him. When the tailor advises Keaton to invest in a new coat, Buster is shocked when he is told it will cost 200 dollars. "I can't afford a new coat!" he objects, "I have hardly any money." Regardless, Buster/The Man saves up his money and purchases the coat, and then notices things have changed for him. People treat him better and elevate him above themselves. When his coat is stolen however, he goes on a downward spiral, messes up the system at work and ends up in prison. Keaton's Man rebels, and takes out the figure of authority, The Chief. Then he wakes up in the tailor's shop, clear that the whole mess has all been a dream. In the real world, the tailor convinces The Man to get his new coat, and he agrees to have it made as some kind of feeble act of revolt.

From his opening scene, Keaton is a natural at drama, but his smooth transition into the serious territory comes as no surprise to seasoned Buster fans, and in fact makes a lot of sense. Though in movies for the technicalities and the thrill of assembling a picture, he was also in it for the laughs. Though he made the globe chuckle with hysteria, he never laughed himself. The key was to always play it straight, to move as few facial muscles as possible. In light of this, a drama such as this seems to be a realistic progression. He applies that Great Stone Face wonderfully and delivers his dialogue like a pro. Lest we forget, Keaton may have made his name in silent films, but at this point he had a couple of decades worth of talkies behind him too. For a man who started on the broad vaudevillian stage fifty years earlier, and connected to his viewers not with words, but with the purity of his own breed of physical language, he excels triumphantly. The story is effective and well written, delivering valid messages on free will and thinking while coming to a conclusion about what freedom really is, but Buster and his subtle efforts are what last in the memory long after viewing.

Fairbanks Jr. was thrilled to be working with the old legend and later stated, "There was quite a lot of discussion and interest in it, and I don't think there was one negative reaction that I could remember for it. I remember everybody praising what Buster did and how he did it. It struck me as a beautiful idea - a novel idea - to put him in a straight part, because he was such a beautiful actor and a great talent. Like any good artist, he would experiment with different ways of reading a line, looking, moving, or interpreting a particular scene. He would try it out and, with the aid of the director [Michael McCarthy], the writers worked out different ideas. He was very creative. He was

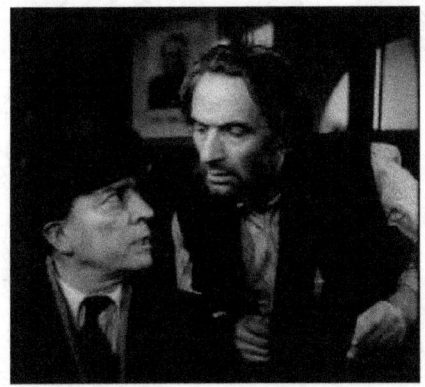 quite an inspiration on all the young people on the set. There was the uniqueness of the story itself, plus the artistry of this great talent which was Keaton. I was one of the many who regarded Keaton as a great artist, and I was so pleased when I was able to convince him to play a serious part in one of my TV movies."

The teleplay script by Laurence B Marcus is tremendous, and provides food for thought in our soulless digital age. It's scattered with brilliant observations and nuggets of social-political satire, but one line in particular stays with me; when Keaton is being trialled and he says, with all the conviction he can muster, "This system which reduces a broken heart to a number in a catalogue". One can only imagine how strong this would have been if fleshed out as a feature length movie. Seeing the mini film as evidence for Keaton's skilled straight acting, The Awakening is extraordinary, and one can only dream about what kind of sub career he might have had if he had landed more dramatic parts on screen.

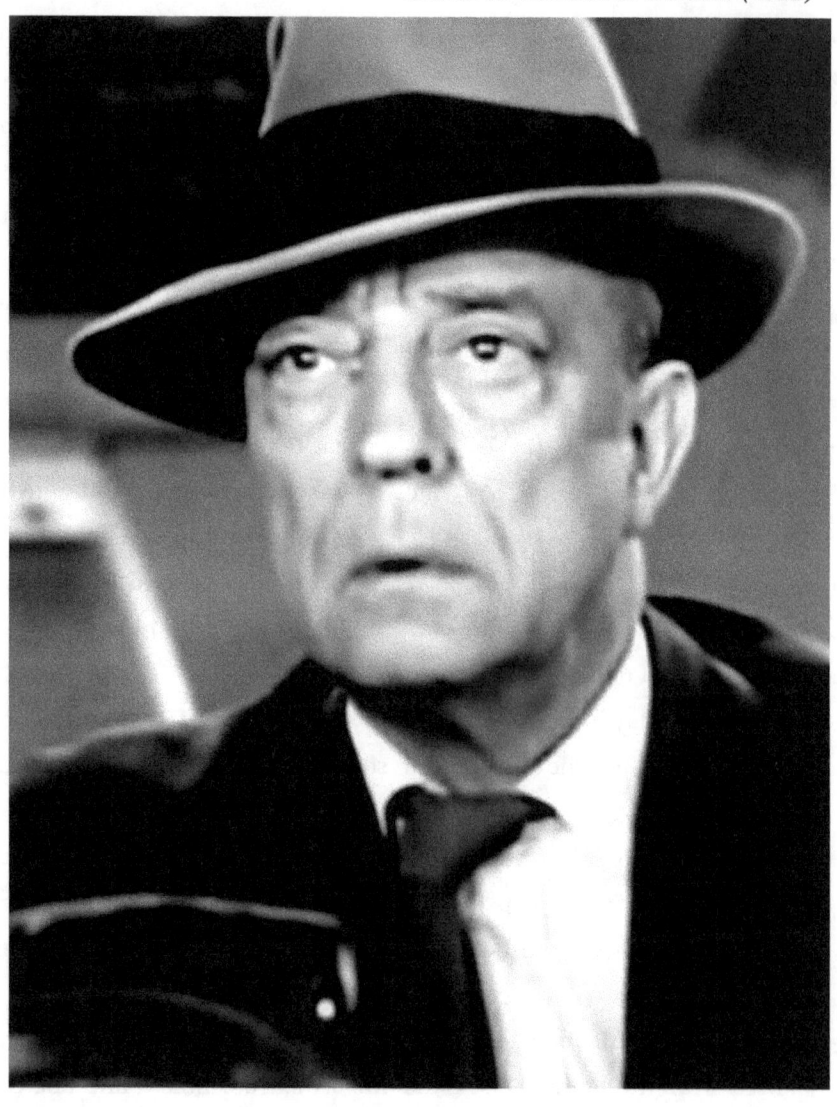

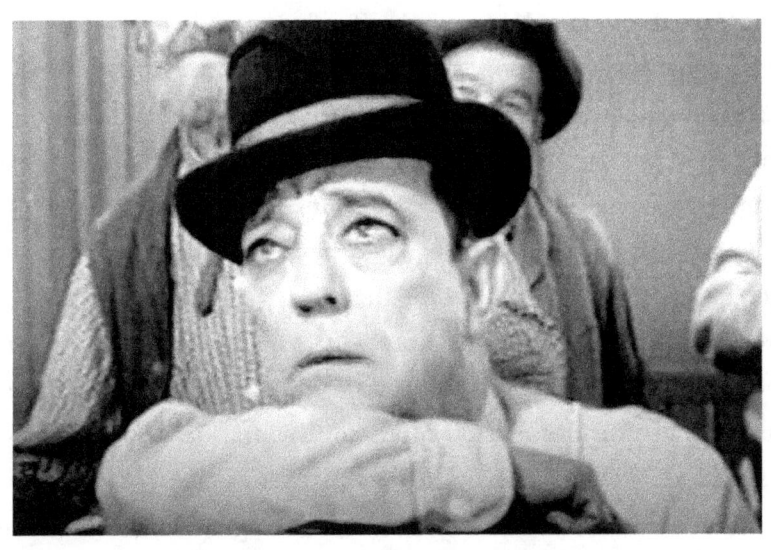

THE SILENT PARTNER

Buster Keaton and the Art of Self Referencing

One thing that was unavoidable for Keaton, one of the last remaining silent film stars not only still working, but totally reachable and accessible, was that he would find himself, quite frequently in fact, referencing his own rich and iconic past. As the decades went on, the silent comedy era grew in reverence, and by the mid 1950s, while most of Buster's classic films were some thirty odd years old, they were firm classics. The silent era was so long ago that it was open for pastiche and parody, not to mention affectionate tribute. Not only that, it was pretty easy for modern filmmakers and TV producers to authentically reproduce the feel and look of the era, even more so when one of its most well known icons was still around, and readily employable.

Of course, Buster didn't mind self referencing his own legacy at all; in fact, he was often more than happy to, at least it seemed that way. After all, he was proud of that work, and spoke fondly, though modestly, of it in various latter day interviews. He had played a crumpled up parody of himself in Sunset Boulevard (a ghost from the past, a has-been, a waxwork),but there were other times where he got to affectionately reproduce the vibe of his golden years, given free reign to move his well known persona into another era and a whole new medium. He was no longer the maker, the director or the conjurer of illusions, but he could doff his flat hat to the days when he was.

One of the more respectful self-referencing credits (this one being close to self examination even) came in 1955 with a little known TV special called Silent Partner. Made for the Screen Director's Playhouse series, and produced by Hal Roach Studios, Silent Partner not only gave Keaton a chance to don his trademark outfit, but also perform a more dramatic role with a fair amount of pathos.

The film begins on Oscar night, as the stars hob-nob and natter as a cheesy TV reporter informs us it's the busiest Oscar night in years. Meanwhile, faded old silent film actor Kelsey Dutton (Buster Keaton) arrives in his favourite bar where the drinkers and the bar man speak of the fakeness of Hollywood. "A bunch of hoke," says one customer. A rather glum Buster sits by the bar. The barman switches on the TV to watch the Oscar ceremony (Buster doesn't care either way if he turns the television on or not), and a bunch of rowdy drinkers come in with a sports trophy, all ready to mock the phony award shindig.

On comes Bob Hope, presenting a "new award" for a respected figure, a movie mogul who has given so much to the motion picture industry. Mr Bale, the respected producer, takes the statuette, steps up to the microphone, and begins a rambling speech. Unexpectedly, he dedicates his award to Kelsey, who covers his face in embarrassment back in the bar. There is then a nicely (and authentically) shot flashback to Dutton's first film role, a chaotic scene involving a ladder and Dutton attempting to save a girl from a house fire. The following scenes illustrate Dutton's natural comic ability, cutting back to the Oscar speech speaking of the decline of Dutton's popularity when the sound era arrived. Now it becomes painfully clear that Buster's own career is being referred to,

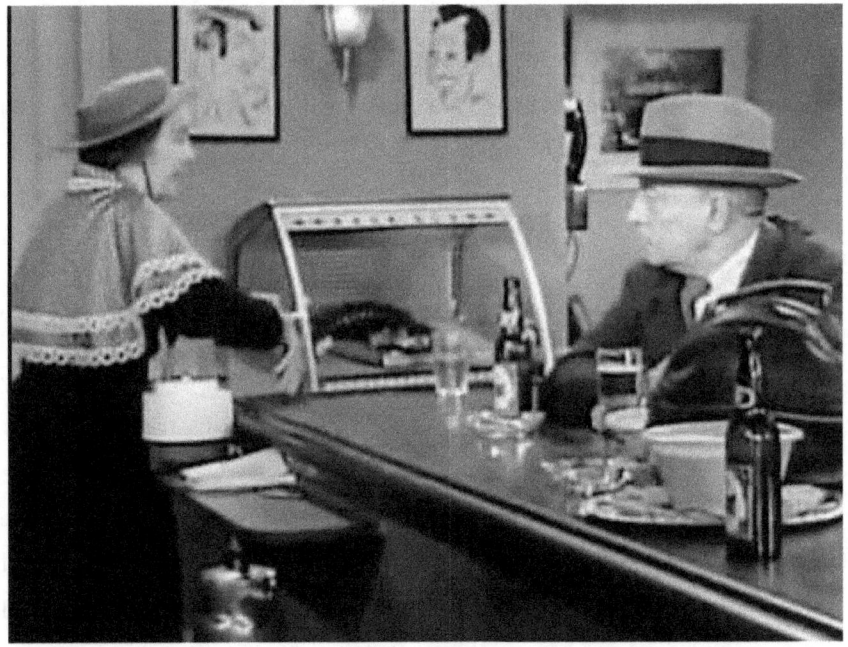

When he finishes his speech, the drinkers mock the ceremony, and say they've never heard of Kelsey Dutton. An ageing customer says Dutton was the biggest star in Hollywood, unaware that she is

standing right beside him. The self-deprecating Dutton does not tell the drinkers he is in fact the star, in true Keaton style being a man with no ego. The ceremony continues, and we are shown more footage of Dutton's classic silent films, with Buster donning a wig for the younger sequences. When the woman in the bar starts to realise Dutton is in the room with her, it takes a completely different turn. All of a sudden the cynicism for the shallowness of the movie world disappears, and Dutton becomes the focal point of the night. When the angriest of the macho drinkers attempts to rough Dutton up, he turns on him and humiliates the half wit. In walks the movie mogul, just at the right moment, to pick up Dutton and take him next door to the ceremony, where they are all eagerly awaiting his arrival. There he will be celebrated as a hero, while the producer hopes to rescue Dutton's flagging career.

Though The Silent Partner is a fun and entertaining quickie, it also has its fair share of sad irony. Buster is playing a variation of himself here, a silent legend long forgotten and tossed aside by Hollywood. There were other ironies too. He just happened to be playing this character, a very Buster creation, on a TV lot owned by Hal Roach, the very man who had led the likes of Laurel and Hardy through the silent glory years. Keaton is excellent in his role, but the silent segments do his legacy little justice. In reality, Keaton's vintage classics were more surreal, much more sophisticated and accomplished than Dutton's. Still, the Dutton scenes are fun and accurate, but only to lesser silent comics, not reflecting the genius of Keaton. The saddest part of it all, of course, is the end, where the movie mogul expresses his gratefulness, and also his regret that the man responsible for his own current status as a respected Hollywood producer, showered with money, praise and awards, is all down to him. If it were not for this forgotten man, the producer suggests, he wouldn't be where he is. Finally showing his gratitude for the man killed by the arrival of the sound era, he promises to revitalise his career. In reality, Hollywood had spat Keaton out, and wouldn't let him near a starring role in a feature film. Guest roles and cameo bit parts were fine, but none of these Hollywood producers trusted Keaton to direct or star in a picture all of his own. The irony cannot have been lost on Keaton, and this egoless genius must have seen how apt it was that he was playing a character in such a predicament on a creaky low budget TV stage.

Still, despite these negative aspects and slightly tragicomic elements, The Silent Partner is one of the best things Keaton did in this era. And to be fair, the sudden appreciation the producer shows him, and promises Hollywood will too, did kind of come true, in a fashion at least. In 1960, he was given an honorary Oscar, a nod of respect to a man who had helped make the movie industry what it was. They would never give him another chance, but could at least pat him on the back and say "Well done, you did good." Buster was touched by the Oscar, and though they had done him wrong in the past, he was big enough to accept it and move on ahead with the rest of his career; not in Hollywood mind you, but on the small screen and the world of independent film. The Silent Partner silently walked away from Hollywood, taking the hint.

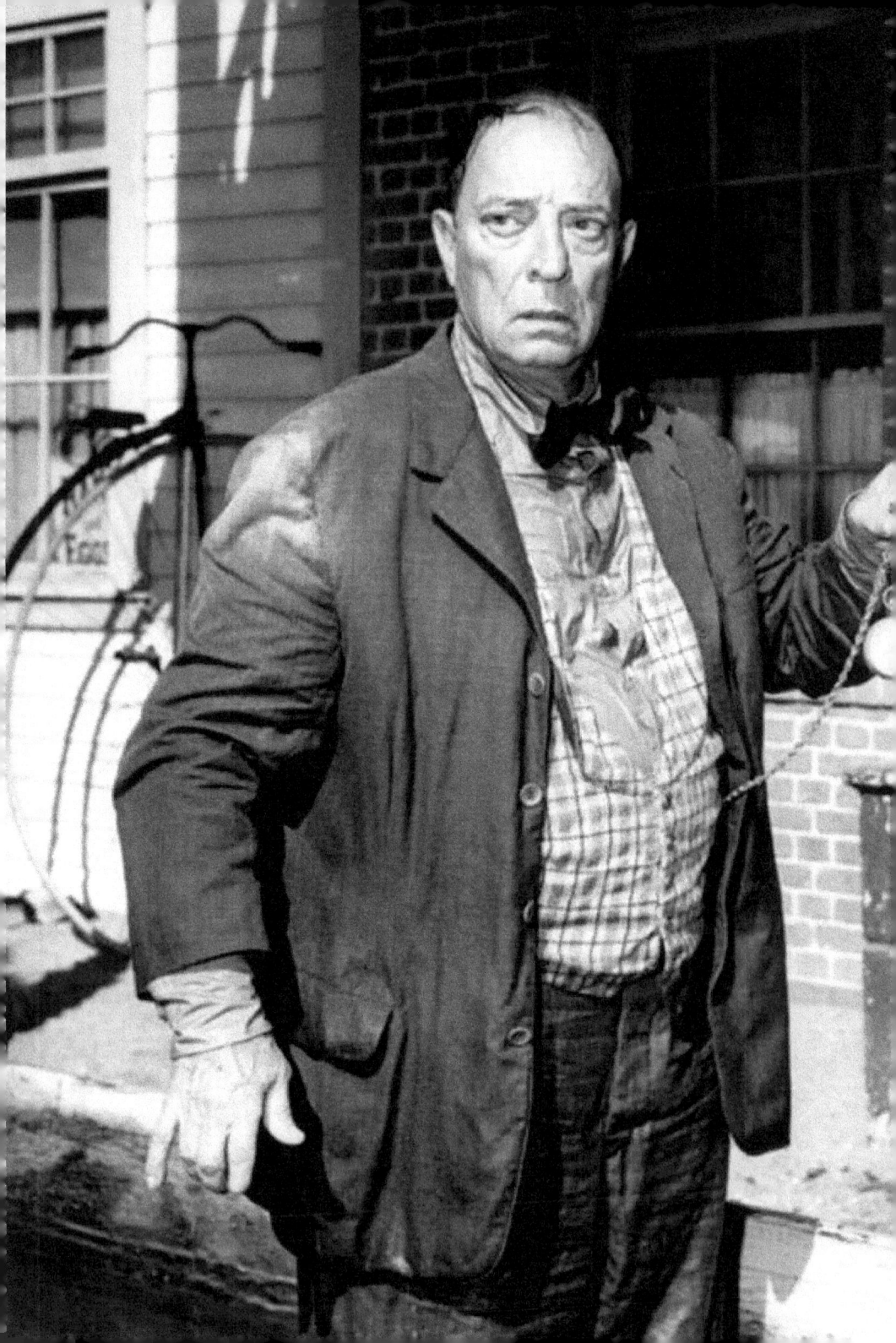

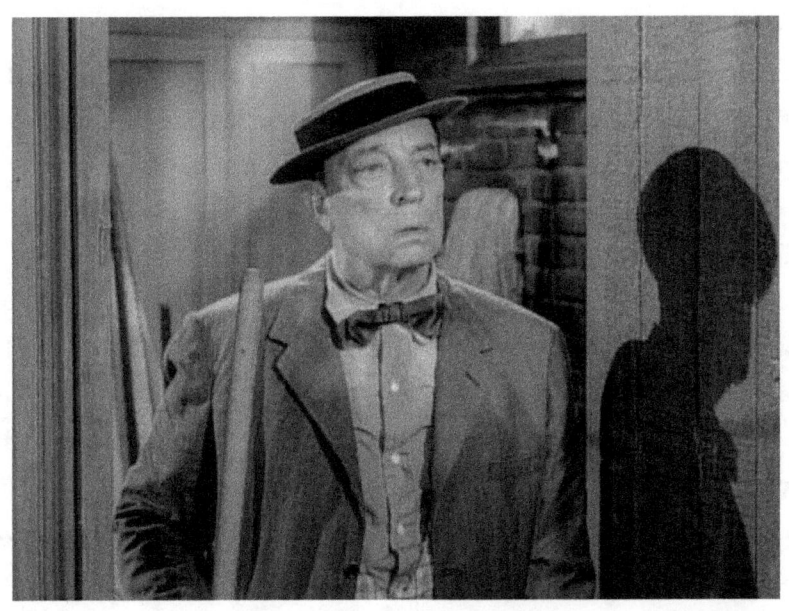

BUSTER AND THE TWILIGHT ZONE

Buster tried a bit of everything in his later years, and surprisingly, some of his most curious, interesting and downright brilliant things were for television. His Candid Camera appearance was genuinely funny, as were his spots on such programs as the Donna Reed Show, but it was when performing in comedic or mildly dramatic roles with a twisted comic edge where he truly excelled. One of Buster's finest TV roles came in 1961, when he starred as Woodrow in Once Upon A Time, a classic episode of The Twilight Zone.

If you don't get a shiver of nostalgia and spooky dread from the opening theme tune and swirling vertigo pattern dizzyingly spinning across the screen as the show starts, then you are probably too young to have ever caught a re-run (or, if you are old enough, an original airing) of this classic sci-fi series. How such a creepy piece of music could be so strangely settling is anyone's guess, but you cannot deny the surreal cosiness one gets from a program such as this. "Your next stop," says the narrator, "the Twilight Zone." And so it begins…

The show starts with some very familiar standard silent film piano music, and footage of a hatted Buster Keaton coming towards the camera. The first caption tells us that our hero is Woodrow Mulligan, a citizen of New York in 1890. The grumpy janitor feels out of place and hates the town and time he lives in. Buster roams the streets wondering what this country is coming to. The black and white cinematography, slightly quickened movements and title cards add to the authenticity, and it's clear that the whole thing is a loving tribute to Keaton's era. Again, he was nodding to his comedic roots, this time in a warmer, more creative manner.

There are jokes worthy of Keaton's classics too. Warned by a policeman about an approaching horse carriage, Keaton turns away, utters a censored expletive, falls into a container of water, and shouts out another censored expletive. Keaton climbs into the basement of his employer, Professor Gilbert, and changes his wet clothes. Fumbling and bumbling in classic Keaton style, it's such a thrill to sit back and relish this latter day slice of comic chaos, a charming little sequence with Buster drying his clothes off and playing an unheard harmonica. He even dries out a wet newspaper ("Hot off the press!") in true mad Keaton style.

Gilbert emerges from a door with a new invention, a time helmet, which he shows to his assistant. Keaton stands in the doorway, curious about this contraption, which will let you travel to any place and any time for 30 minutes. When Gilbert and his right hand man go off to celebrate with a glass of champagne, Buster enters the room, looks around shiftily, and tries the metal hat on. Gazing in a mirror, he poses a little then twists some knobs. It catches fire, and in a fit of panic Keaton runs down the road, trouserless I might add, and is suddenly sent to modern times with a huge explosion. Gone are the horse drawn carriages, replaced by noisy road diggers and speeding cars, the old worldly silence drowned away by traffic humming, yelling drivers and heavy drilling. Keaton, still without trousers, has his time travel hat stolen by a kid, and in a hilarious scene, chases him down a busy street trying to retrieve it, catching the attention of a local cop.

Tired out, Buster stops and gets on the back of a push bike, but the cop is in hot pursuit. As the troubles mount, Buster/Woodrow realises that 1960 is just as bad as 1890, worse in fact. When he breaks the hat, he realises he is trapped. In the company of a scientist with a thorough interest in Woodrow's era, the janitor takes his broken device to a repair shop. The two men end up going back together, both having a newfound realisation of their own. The scientist realises his hopes for the 1890 will not be fulfilled, and that the period is not what he expected, while Buster returns with a fresh perspective and admiration for his time.

This really is a lovely little homage to the silent era, and a genuinely funny and entertaining story in its own right. There is also an interesting point raised about people longing to be elsewhere, and finding that their desired destination (in this case, their desired time) is not what they expected. (Woody Allen would later explore this idea in his 2009 film Midnight in Paris.) Most of all though, one comes away most impressed by Keaton, whose work here is very special indeed, both a wildly comic portrait of a misplaced man, and a loving nod to his own past.

Keen eyed Busterites will also spot his infamous amputated finger. When he was three he got it caught in a clothes wringer (yes, Buster had the best parents in the world) and in this episode he gets the same finger caught in a clothes wrong.

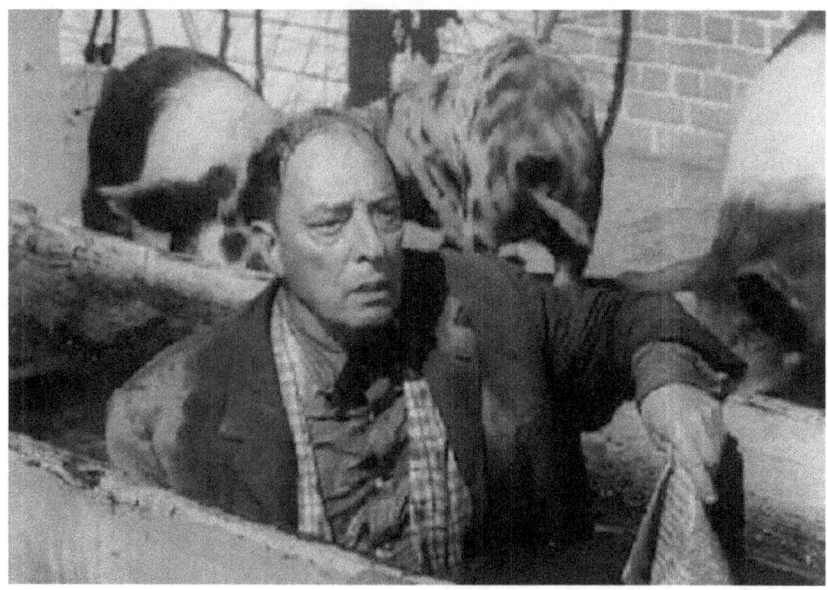

These days, the episode is considered a classic, and it regularly comes up as a highlight from his latter period. Some people have chosen to look at it the wrong way though. The AV Club published a strange piece in regards to Buster's performance, and by the look of things hadn't seen a post-silent Keaton picture at all, so surprised they are by Buster's elderly appearance. Fatally hung up on his classic work, they become ageist, and fail to see the realities of the ageing process, even in an immortal screen idol of Keaton's fame.

"Buster Keaton was in his mid-sixties when he starred in Once Upon A Time, and it shows," they began. "Go back and watch his best films, like Sherlock Jr. or The General, he seems like a statue granted impossible grace, a stone-faced human of elegant construction constantly at odds with his environment. Chaplin made his humanity his calling card, but there's something almost alien about Buster Keaton at the height of his powers. He's like Data, the android from Star Trek: The Next Generation: a being of astonishing gifts who is nonetheless constantly thwarted by the demands of the day to day. He was his own best special effect, and his stunts are legendary even today."

They continue: "But look at him in Once Upon A Time, and the first emotion you'll probably feel is shock, with maybe a little horror thrown in for extra cruelty. Time makes fools of us all, sure, and it's not like a wrinkled face and a sagging belly are anything to be ashamed about. It's just the contrast is so goddamn stark. Keaton was never able to make much of a go during the sound age, so there are fewer visual documents of him going from young and perfect to old and busted. But even without the suddenness of the transition, Keaton still doesn't look well. This is a man who once hung over waterfalls and rode in bicycle seats and let houses fall on him, and now he's shuffling up the boardwalk like a granddad somebody forgot at the mall. The fact that Keaton died of lung cancer five years after this was filmed isn't much of a twist ending. Yet Once Upon A Time is meant as pure, goofy pleasure, and it's a testament to Keaton's strength as a performer (and his willingness to do just about anything for a laugh) that the contrast between the performer's shattered visage and the episode's whimsical tone never really comes into play. While there's not a hint of sadness or gloom in Once Upon A Time, looking back on it now, it's hard not to be a little sad. The moral is, you should stay in your place, which isn't all that great as morals go, and it's even worse when you realize what

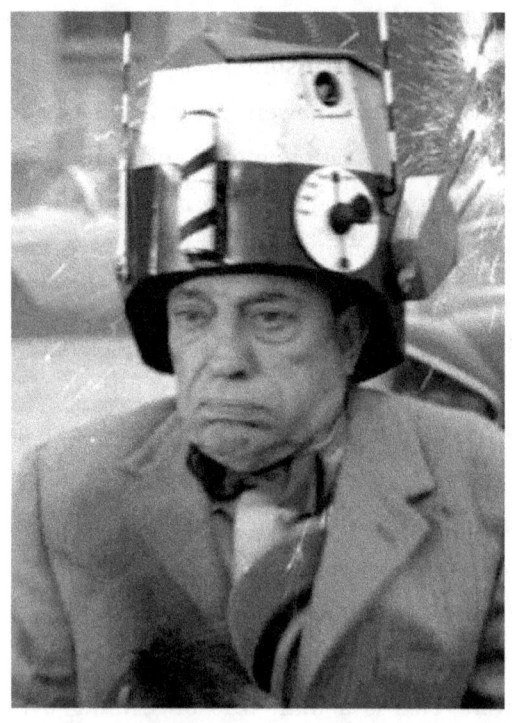 that meant for Keaton, and how his inability to transition from silent to talking motion pictures destroyed the latter half of his career. The more I think about it, as great as Keaton is in this, he looks undeniably tired; not in a soul-searing, last legs kind of a way, but just going through the routines without all the flair they once had. Because the truth of the matter is, as much as we'd like to find that one year, that one town, that one moment that fits us better than any other, things are always rushing forward, and there's no special helmet to set the dial back."

Anyone reading this would get the totally wrong idea about Buster's later years. Cruel to the point of insulting, such writers make a mockery of the fact that Keaton did not stay stick thin and eternally youthful in his sixties. These pieces reinforce the myth of Keaton being a spent force, a clumsy old comic spoofing his former glories in unworthy surroundings. We all love a gossipy tale, especially one of a Hollywood icon and his doomy down fall, but with Keaton it's not quite as simple as that, or as tragic. All careers have ups and downs, but if anything, Buster's aged appearance made him all the more human, all the more real, and it has to be said, all the more funny. On top of that, he wasn't lowering himself or having to perform in a way he didn't wish to. It was a continuation, once again, of the old Buster, consistent and true to his image, even in a 1960s sci-fi series.

Other writers "get" it though. Film School Rejects, though finding the episode silly, had to admit that Buster was fantastic. "And who do you get to guest star when half your episode is done as a silent film? Buster Keaton," they wrote. "Not a bad choice. Keaton is such a force that even at the ripe old age of 66, he's still the brightest part of this completely silly story."

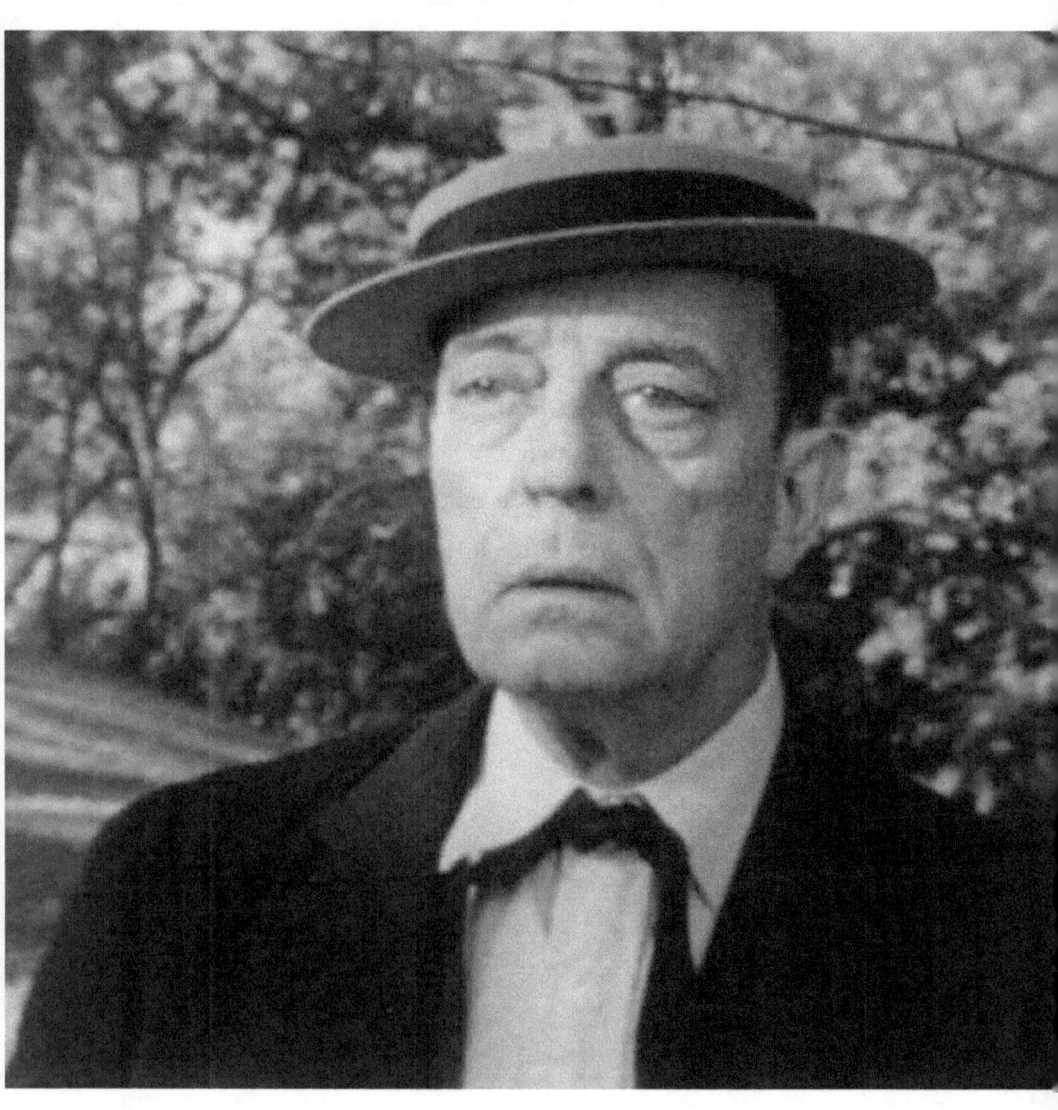

Keaton in 1960's The Devil to Pay

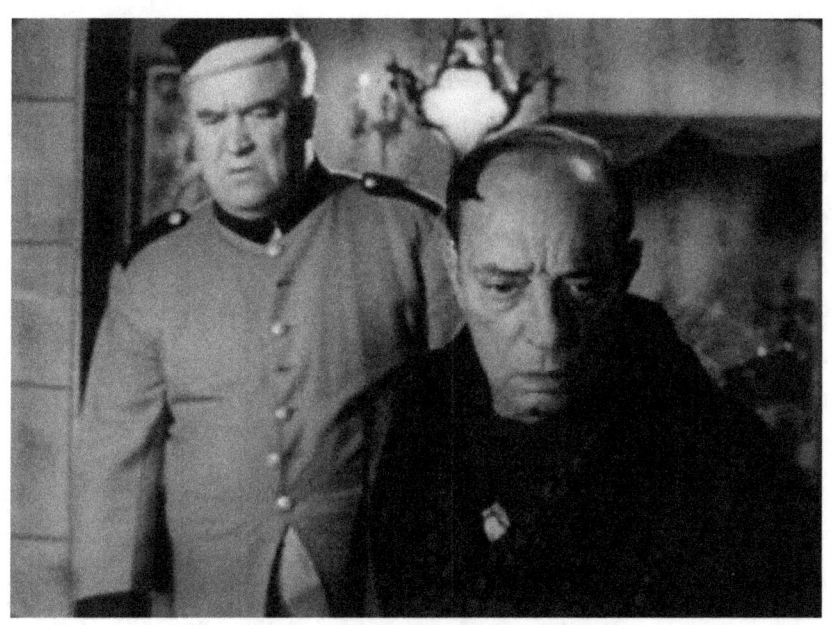

THE DEVIL TO PAY

Dusting Off A Lost Curiosity

As the years go by and Buster's death become further and further away, his career seems to make more sense as a whole, rather than as a fractured mess with shards separating the eras. That huge on-screen time line spans half a century, and goes through the silent era, Hollywood's glamorous golden age (though he was sidelined in it), the advent of TV, the changing sixties and the arrival of the avant-garde. While many will jump straight to The General and his other glory works, the internet has made it possible that over looked and long forgotten oddities have come to light. And one of these, no

97

doubt, is the odd ball curiosity The Devil to Pay, a short which Buster starred in at the turn of the 1960s.

Most people would more than likely hop straight past The Devil to Pay, but there is something about these surreal oddities in Buster's final years that really appeal to me. Made in 1960 for the National Association of Wholesalers, this strange industrial film features an odd ball plot about a NASA rocket accidentally landing on the devil's flower garden. With a synopsis like this, who wouldn't want to investigate closer?

Devil to Pay is one of the most overlooked and forgotten pieces of film Buster ever did, but in truth this weird little gem is well worth 30 minutes of your time, and bits of it feel close to his legendary two-reelers. The grainy film starts with a cheap title card reading "Buster Keaton in - The Devil to Pay", accompanied by a drawing of Satan and some creepy organ music. The story begins, our narrator tells us, in Cape Canaveral, with the launch of a troublesome second rocket launch, Explorer 2. "It thundered off in first class fashion," he says, but the radio went down and NASA wondered what the heck had happened to it. It turns out the rocket ended up in Hades, a planet ruled by a man named Diablos, played by Buster. We first see this villainous fiend tending to his garden in a silk robe, watering his plants before going inside and dusting off an altar he keeps for an old flame. Accompanied by classic silent movie style piano, we follow the disturbing sentimentality of this formerly evil leader. His followers long for his old vitality.

When the picture of his old love tilts, he uses special powers to re configure it and gets ready to nap. Suddenly there is a shattering earthquake and Buster goes into a panic, hiding under the bed while his servant sees what's caused the fuss. It's the arrival of the elusive space craft, which has crashed on to Buster's beloved flower bed. Raising up his courage, Buster emerges from under the safety of the bed and is shown the devastation. The Great Stone Face looks troubled, saddened by the destruction and moved by the lowly image of one sole surviving flower. He plucks it up carefully, close to sobbing, and seems confused by the USA logo on the crashed module. The evil leader goes inside and checks out his globe of planet Earth. "The people of the USA had better watch out" exclaims the narrator as Buster dons his evil satanic get up, a costume which looks more ludicrous than truly evil, adding to the off beat hilarity of the film. With staff in hand, he and his loyal servant prepare for their mission. Buster then adopts his trademark outfit (flat hat and dapper get up) and launches himself off in a rocket, peering through the round window as he elevates into space, declaring war on the USA.

Buster crash lands, vengeance on his mind, and starts to explore the new terrain. This sentimental journey back to the capital of the United States has Buster bumbling along the streets, attracting the attention of suspicious police officers, and despite being in his sixties, taking some fabulous pratfalls. He listens in on a woman's speech going on in the woodlands, gets into bother with them, then joins their liberated fight to "eliminate the middle man," this meaning the country's many wholesalers.

Keaton then excels at being Keaton, falling into a lift and down some stairs as he might have done in his glory years (this whole section is definitely a homage to his classic films). He tries to get some sleep but finds it hopeless (no wonder, with that ear slaughtering organ on the soundtrack!), the irritating voice of the

99

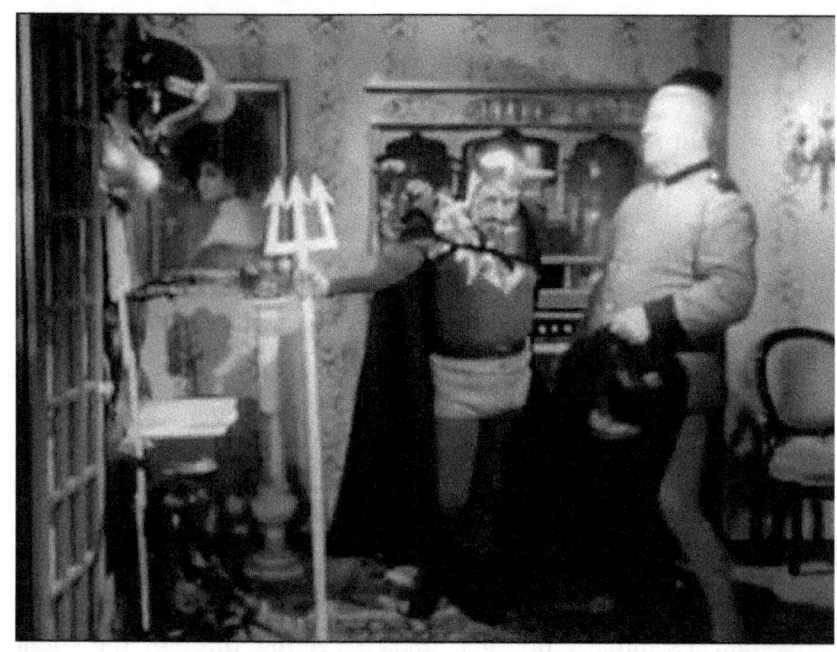

speaker echoing in his ears. He gets up in his nighty and uses his powers to wake the pesky woman up in her bed, then manages to finally get off to sleep himself, while everyone in the country awakes to write the words "Eliminate the Middleman" in a zombified state, then, clad in their pyjamas and robes, mail it into the mail box.

The mail industry goes into a frenzy, as does the wholesaling market. "Suddenly there were a million little orders to fulfil rather than a thousand big ones." Without wholesalers, the county goes into complete meltdown. It is here we remember that The Devil to Pay was an industrial film made by the Wholesalers Association. The film is clever in this way; 15 minutes in, we have been so busy enjoying ourselves in Keaton's presence that we forgot all about the message of the film. As an endorsement for Wholesalers, it really does its job, though the stiff middle section jars terribly with Keaton's wonderful scenes. Still, though boring, it makes you realise how important wholesaling is in the great consumerist rat race. The film starts to look like a piece of brainwashing, with the nation reduced to a wreck in an apocalyptic breakdown of society and trade. "There was the Devil to Pay" booms our dramatic story teller.

In the end, the same women who so despised the middle men long for the wholesaler, wishing again for the time when bargains were possible due to bulk buying and distribution. It seems that earth will quite literally turn to hell without accessible consumerism. The women then convince Keaton to zombify the nation again, this time into writing a letter to congress about restoring the wholesalers.

The Devil to Pay may seem like an odd film to devote so much time to, but its dated and tiresome wholesale preaching aside, the movie features some of Buster's funniest scenes from the latter period, and they are directed wonderfully by Herb Skoble. It seems unfortunate that Keaton should be given the chance to shine as an older man in the strangest of circumstances. Though merely given seconds at a time in the mainstream, and forced to go along with terrible scripts, in these obscure shorts and industrial films Keaton was free to do what he did best - be Buster Keaton, pure and simple. The Devil to Pay is indicative that he could shine in any surroundings.

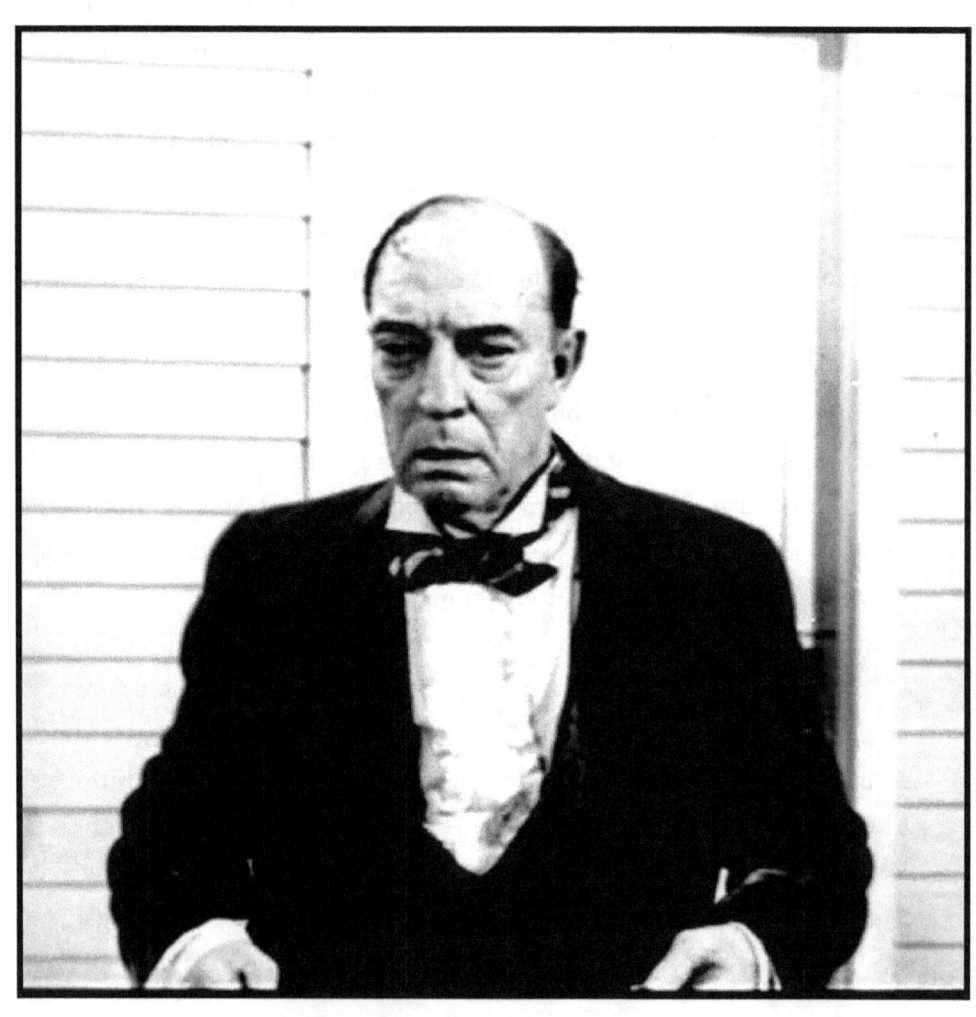

Lester Snapwell

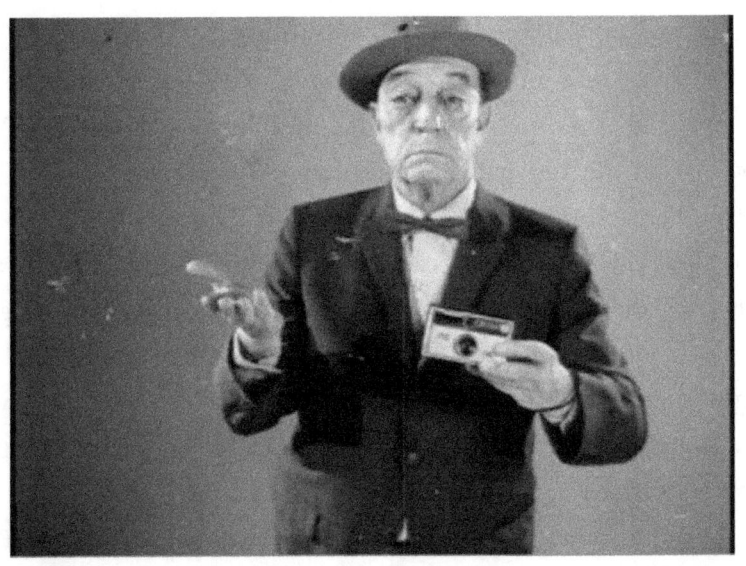

THE TRIUMPH OF LESTER SNAPWELL

Buster Keaton, amidst the TV roles and Hollywood cameos which left a lot to be desired, ended up in another odd ball industrial film in 1963 called The Triumph Of Lester Snapwell. Seen as minor Keaton (this being lesser Keaton in what many regard as his lesser era, which makes the film very minor indeed) it's actually a charming, low budget glimpse into the past, commissioned by the Eastman Kodak company. It's good as a history lesson on the development of the camera, but these days is more of an opportunity to catch a glimpse of a let loose Buster Keaton.

Basically an extended, slightly self indulgent advert for how great Kodak was in the 1960s, it stars Buster as Lester, a photographer having a spot of bother capturing his love, Clementine, in photograph. Garish in colour and brilliantly soundtracked (very sixties in its use of harsh organ and wind instrumentation), it conjures up the mid 1800s wonderfully, with Keaton looking fabulous as the top hatted Lester, who clearly worships his girl. Setting her up in a graceful pose by an old Penny Farthing bike, he struggles with his ancient camera for a spell, and finds his shot ruined by the arrival of a rather unphotographic woman, the girl's mother, and the limitations of his technology. Lester tries with all his might to capture the image, but ends up setting the mother in law on fire. She chases him off in a rage, and as he goes flying through a door, he is killed.

Lester awakes in a smoky room, where a bearded Father Time offers him the chance to take the perfect picture, catapulting him firstly to 1888 where the camera has advanced with the arrival of the

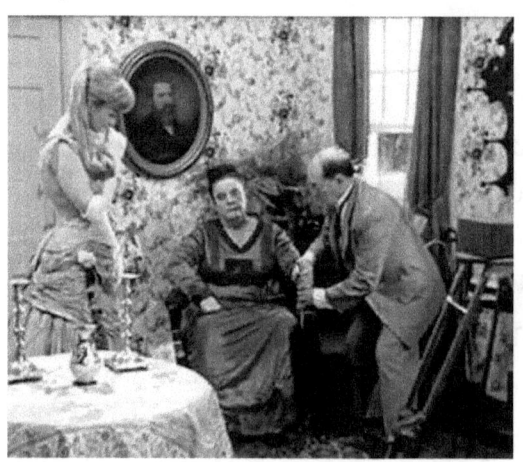 first Kodak camera. Keaton, now dressed in fitting 1880s togs, assembles his camera, follows the instructions and heads out to capture something on film. He spots a passing parade in the street and snaps away, but finds

himself forced into using his final frame on a passing police officer. However he outsmarts the copper by running away, saving his last picture for sweet Clementine. Again though, he finds it more troublesome than he had envisioned. Setting the scene perfectly, he clumsily uses his last frame while cleaning the lens. "Don't move, I'll be right back," he says, heading across to Rochester to reload his film. Arriving back in the very Keaton-esque manner of a sliding fall, two months on and Keaton has more film to photograph Clementine. But it all goes wrong again, and the mother in law sends him on his way, where he smashes a window and make a prat of himself.

He visits Father Time again, and is transported to the Roaring Twenties, where the camera has taken on leaps and bounds technologically. Loading up his new device, a fairly mundane activity which is dragged out and made half interesting by Keaton's movements and the authentic twenties soundtrack which comes bursting from the speakers, Snapwell ends up making a pig's ear of the whole thing. Glumly he takes a seat, but a mysterious hand appears through the door and passes him a gift - a make up set for Clementine. Donning a garish fur coat, Buster heads out with his ukulele, and a classic Keaton hat. When he gets to Clementine's home, a couple of burly delivery men nearly beat him up when he sits and tries out the make up. He gives the set to Clementine and gets his camera all ready for the big picture. However, he messes up again, and Lester finds himself in the presence of Father Time once more.

Buster finds himself, suited and hatted, in the late fifties, with Clementine looking every bit the housewife of the era. Now without the pesky flash powder, Lester ends up breaking the camera, and messing up all over again. Father Time then takes him forward to 63 with the latest Kodak in his grasp. The following section is a glowing endorsement for the then latest model of Kodak camera, much simpler than what Lester has been used to. He ends up in a room with a gang of beauties, who are unfortunately for Buster sent to the door by Clementine and her mother. Finally, Lester has achieved his goal, decent pictures of Clementine. Of course Lester's real triumph, and the pay off for the whole film. comes when he tricks the mother in law into a pool, and makes off with Clementine.

Though much slower paced than much of Keaton's vintage work, The Triumph of Lester Snapwell is wonderfully made for an elongated advert, and Keaton is excellent in his role. Only performing a couple of clownish falls here and there, he holds the film together with something much harder to pull off. At this point, after following Keaton's career through nearly fifty years of work, ups and downs, clunkers and masterpieces, he's become a kind of cosy presence, someone we could watch and enjoy doing anything. Even a rather dated 30 minute advert for Kodak cameras becomes a fascinating historical document, a glimpse into another technological era (long before smart phone cameras and the digital age) and the winding down of a massive career. Even in these unremarkable circumstances, Keaton is fabulous, and as Lester Snapwell (one of his most overlooked characters, who could have had his own series in my book) Buster is the underdog we root for.

Most Keaton books overlook or totally ignore this picture, which is probably understandable (I am sure more people would like to read about Sherlock Jr. or The Navigator than this), but also a shame, as anyone who takes the time to study it might be surprised by its merits, the most vital of which for me remains Keaton's measured effort.

It's hard to find anyone who is remotely fond of the Snapwell saga, but a blog entitled Fallen Rocket seemed to share my views on the lost oddity. "This might sound weird to say, but I think this is the most successful of any of Buster's late-career works that try to mimic silent films," they write. "It's still done with a bit of a wink to old-timey sensibilities, but the comedy feels more genuine. I'm guessing Buster got a fair amount of input on the gags, not necessarily because of the gags themselves, but because of the way they build – they get set up nicely, knowing when to come unexpectedly and when to get foreshadowed to create a bigger laugh. And there's some nice ones here. Buster playing around with the 19th century camera is a hoot, and there's a fantastic mishap involving his girlfriend's mother and a photographic plate. The modern-day segment has some amusing gags too, along with the sight gag of little-fellow Buster being flanked by statuesque models. (Who knew a Kodak camera was such a babe magnet?)"

Anyone taking the time to dig through this less celebrated era of Buster's career will be rewarded and pleasantly surprised by this. Might learn a thing or two about cameras too.

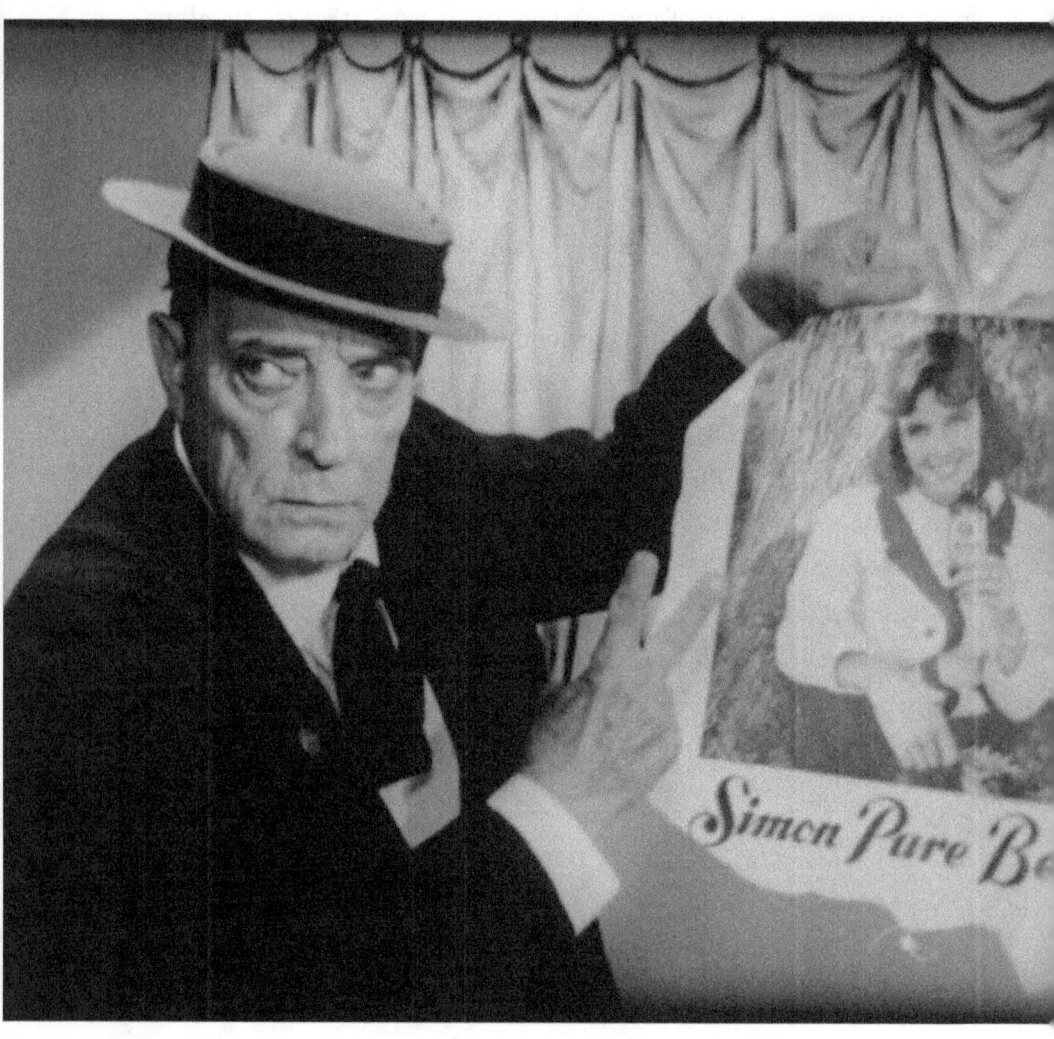

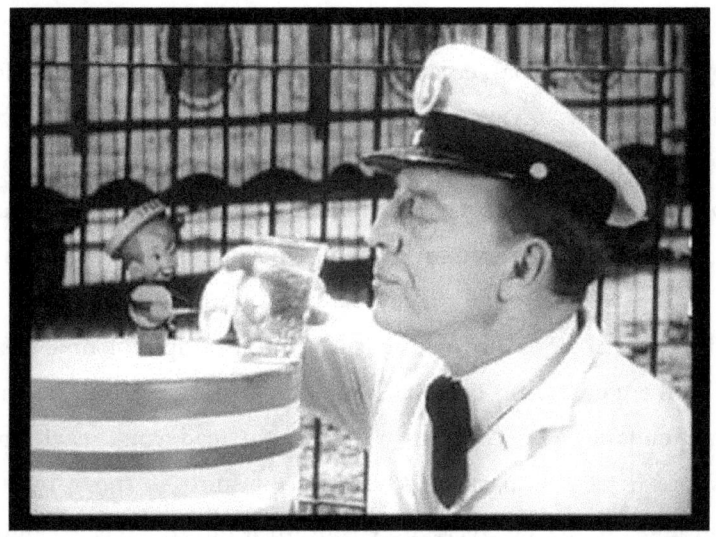

BUSTER KEATON: AD MAN

*"It's easy work for me, I do 'em quick,
I stay home here and enjoy life."*

Like any other working pro, Buster took what he could, and as long as he could retain his dignity and still live the Buster Keaton persona (flat hat, clownish walk, dapper get up), then the work was good, and Buster could get the best out of the given situation. With his TV work rising throughout the 1950s, Keaton was adopted for a new medium that tied in with his small screen shenanigans - TV advertising. Buster was perfect for this, a familiar face, an icon in fact, who wasn't overly expensive, was a true professional and someone the viewers could relate to. He began appearing in TV adverts to boost his income, and though some people balked at the very idea (TV itself was considered low, let alone TV advertising) these ads are interesting, often very funny, and the ones that survive at least, really do offer a lot to the Keaton visual canon. Short, snappy and broad, they were closer to his early two-reeler classics than anything he got to do in the movies, that's for sure.

His advert for Firebird petrol is a prime example of how Keaton could make comic gold out of a simple endorsement. Buster plays a pump attendant trying to fill up a car, but the lead won't reach up the hill where the car is parked. When the car starts to move by itself, Keaton and the driver chase after it down a hill. It's like an outtake from Seven Chances, a brilliantly filmed little scene which results in the car reaching the pump perfectly, where Keaton catches up to it and starts to fill her up. He gives the camera an exhausted look. Unlike other adverts of this era, Buster's are all funny, nicely filmed and neatly wrapped little short films in their own right.

Buster did a great commercial for Milky Way in 1961, the best chocolate in all the galaxy straight from mars. In his familiar get up Buster stands before a giant billboard advertising Milky Way, but every time he turns away the cartoon cow comes to life and dances along to the ad's jingle. When Buster turns back, the cow stands still. A baffled Buster tries to outsmart the cow, creeping behind the board and peeping round slowly. The cow moos in Buster's face and knocks him back. Cue the irresistible tagline: "There's so much milk in a milky way you can almost hear it moo."

The Great Stone Face applies his trademark blank face (too sad eyed to be truly emotionless) brilliantly to the wide eyed, highly nostalgic advert. With such results, and the fact that Keaton was making money from such ventures, makes you wonder why anyone would slam him taking on a bit of advertising work (easy money) in his sixties.

His ad for Ford is also a classic. Only a minute long, it features Buster on a ladder painting a sign above a bridge, held up there by car which when speeds off, knocks poor Buster off the ladder and a tin of paint on the driver's head. With frantic silent movie piano music and dated, harsh narration, the ad is not as well timed and put together as some of the others he did, but it was at least in keeping with his legendary persona. Keaton shot this in 1965, only a matter of months before his death. The fact he looks so well makes his impending demise all the more unfathomable.

Keaton posed for some still vodka poster ads and billboards, but he also filmed a couple of commercials for Simon Pure Beer. These are my personal favourites. From the opening second, Simon Pure ensure that they utilise the best of Keaton, and certainly get their moneys worth. In one ad, they present Keaton before a black chalk board, where Buster (in his usual hat and waist coat combo) draws a beer pump in chalk and proceeds to pour himself a glass. He then chalks on a chair and table, on to which he reclines, before picking up his beer and a newspaper. It's a little gem, and an advert definitely deserving of the man.

Simon Pure Beer seem to be the guys who knew how to use Keaton the best. In another ad he is sitting on a bench with a newspaper which keeps on folding out, getting larger and larger, until it becomes so big it knocks him off his seat and on to the ground. It's a nod to a gag he did in 1921's High Sign, but rather than appearing desperate, it gives you a warm glow. Thankfully, Keaton is faced with an advert for Simon Pure Beer amidst the gigantic newspaper, which gives him an idea - to take a girl out for a beer and a nice meal. The final gag comes with the arrival of the menu, which

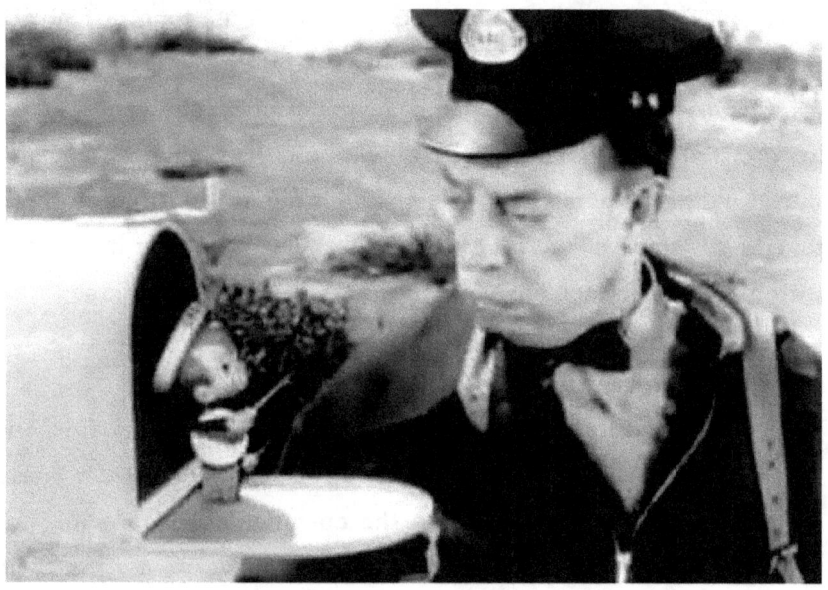

to Buster's horror, like the newspaper, keeps on unfolding.

His 1958 ads for Alka Seltzer remain possibly the best known Keaton commercials. One involves him as a tired ship captain at the wheel (a nod to The Navigator) feeling a bit worse for wear. The narrator says he has an aching head, and Buster, speaking in that deep, gravelly voice of his, adds "and an iceberg straight ahead." Then a little ship's mate appears by his side (a puppet), informing Buster that he needs a pick me up, some Alka Seltzer. "Bless that relief giving Alka Seltzer," Buster says, later reclining on a chair with a blanket over him.

Buster did another advert for Alka Seltzer, where he is seen at a party over indulging, and then feeling rather poorly at his bed side at night. "I'll feel worse in the morning," he says, just as the little puppet child comes to his aid once again. Buster swallows the Seltzer, and the next day he is done up in top hat and tails, striding care free and fit as a fiddle down the street. He removes his hat, revealing a packet of Alka Seltzer underneath. "Always carry Alka Seltzer" Buster advises us.

The only problem with these particular ads, as charming as they are, is that they decline to use Buster to his full abilities. Getting him to merely look a bit fed up, then down the drink with a quick little corny endorsement line, the makers of the adverts have, in some ways, wasted the talents of a comic genius. No pratfalling, no bumbling, no surreal gags. Still, Buster pulls them off, and even when chatting away to a puppet, he keeps his dignity intact.

The best Alka Seltzer ad is the one where he plays the mountie who's spent three years tracking down a villain. Feeling ill once again, he collapses in the rocks. But fear not, the singing puppet pops up from behind a rock and saves the day with his Alka Seltzer. Harmless stuff, but Keaton has so little to do it seems a pity.

There is another, more notable Alka Seltzer ad too, this one referencing (subtly) some of his classic work. Buster plays a mail man delivering his last letter, but the house turns out to be a mobile home on wheels, which drives away before he can post the letter. "HEY!" yells Buster, suddenly feeling off it. Of course, right on cue comes the helpful puppet and his "wonderful" song, which a few adverts in I am sure Buster was tired of hearing. The best visual gag in the whole Alka Seltzer ad campaign comes at the end of this particular commercial, when Buster rides a motorbike and catches up with the motor home, posting it through the window as he passes by. Of course, he has the Alka Selter to thank for this small victory.

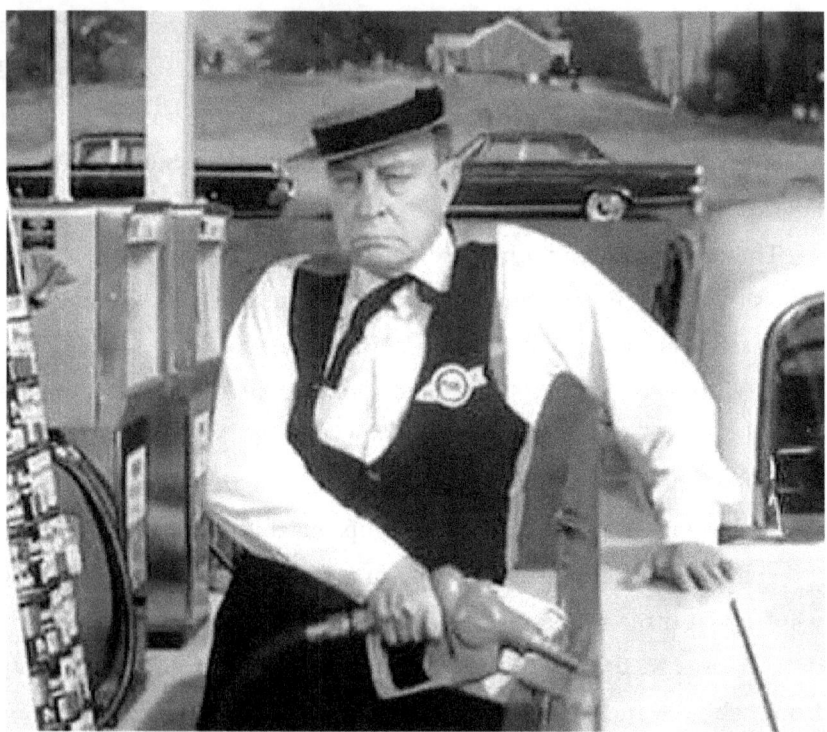

Thanks to the internet, many obscure adverts from this period have resurfaced. One is a 1960 slot for Jeep automobiles, which features Keaton on a trampoline, bouncing gleefully a few times before going up and not coming down. Rather bizarrely, it turns out Buster got stuck in a giant bird's nest. What this has to do with jeeps though, is anyone's guess.

While it's obvious why some people pity former stars "reduced" to plugging products on TV for pay cheques, there are a few things that need to be taken into consideration before getting too critical. Firstly it depends on how much the star is getting paid for this easy, quick work. Secondly, it depends what they are plugging. And thirdly, it all comes down to what they are expected to do. Orson Welles often lowered himself to adverts that were belittling, whether it be frozen peas or Paul Mason wine. Often pissed himself when narrating these ads, Orson despised them, but they paid well and all that was required was for him to don his best "Orson Welles" voice, that golden tone so good at narrating anything from a quick plug to a Roman epic. That said, few of Orson's commercials are worth much today, and are interesting on a more novel level.

Buster's ads however, are brilliant. He is given a script in each one, yes, but seems free to use his iconic look and persona to its best effect, at least for the most part. There is no degradation, and if anything, it was good for Buster's profile and bank balance, which he was re-building in the 50s and 60s. Lumping as many of Buster's commercials together as one can smites down any theories that he had somehow lowered himself. Like quick comedy sketches he did on TV, they are an important facet to his latter period, and fans find them naively appealing, and rather heart warming. It proved also how strong Buster's image was.

Rather than seeing them as an aid in his supposed downfall, I choose to see them as a vital part of his development, and proof that this old veteran could survive the changing times. He was still employable decades on as an old man, more than willing to play the game and keep his eye on the ball. The game just happened to be TV advertising, but in his own way, he showed us what could be done, simply and cheaply, in that most sidelined and overlooked art form.

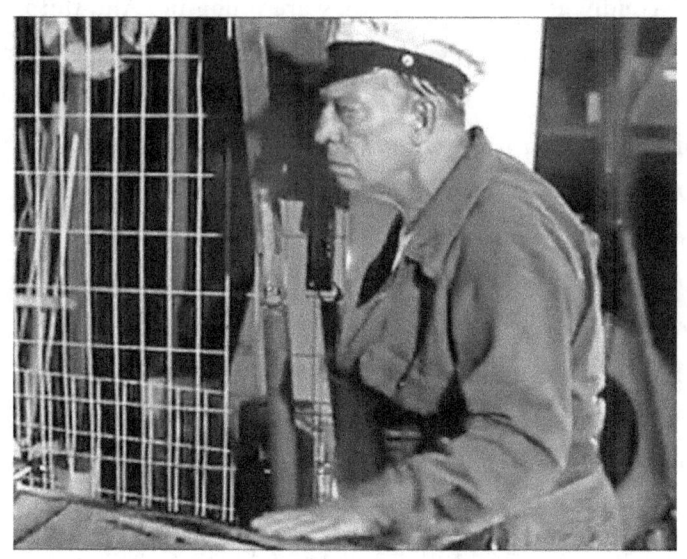

ALONG FOR THE RIDE

Buster As Swinging Sixties Bit Parter

The 1960s were a very interesting time for Keaton. He began the decade with various short films, TV appearances and commercials. As the years went by though, Buster suddenly became visible to a whole new breed of filmmakers, and many various types I might add. Though none of them gave Buster a lead or truly sizeable role in their varied productions, he did land some notable cameos and bit parts. None of these parts could hope to match the work he had done decades earlier, nor the admittedly brilliant short two-reelers and off the wall experiments he did in the final year of his life, but they gave

Buster steady work and plenty of interesting, and often very strange, things to do.

One of his first credits of the 1960s was Michael Cutiz's version of The Adventures of Huckleberry Finn, in which Buster played a lion tamer. Released by MGM, it proved to be his final role for the company, with whom he had endured a troubled and rather mixed relationship. A largely forgotten film, one of its saving graces is the brief appearance of Buster. The first colour filming of the well loved story, it featured, besides Keaton, an all star cast. But Keaton, working for MGM for the first time since his 1949 film In the Good Old Summertime, coasts through his bit part. The actor playing Huck, Eddie Hodges, recalled working with Keaton with fondness years later. "I had had my fill of I-hate-kids types and could smell 'em a mile away. Mr. Keaton treated me as an equal. He was kind and very gentle with this young and thirsty skill of mine."

Keaton also appeared n the all star comedy feast, It's A Mad Mad Mad Mad World, released in 1963. Directed by Stanley Kramer, the comedy classic features a dazzling cast of famous faces all in pursuit of $350,000. Spencer Tracy, Sid Caeser and Mickey Rooney are just some of the names who feature in this who's who of legendary comedy, and though Keaton's part is small, he makes an impression all the same. A guest appearance it may have been but his scene as Jimmy remains a memorable one. One can only wonder how the film might have turned out had Keaton been given the role they originally had lined up for him, Smiler, which ironically went to his old sparring partner, Jimmy Durante. Interestingly, there is a cut scene featuring Buster and Spencer Tracy, but the finished edit has very little Keaton, much less than desired it has to be said.

These small roles were basically cameos and little else, given to Buster as a mark of respect and appreciation. But these castings were often wasted, and few of thee filmmakers seemed to grasp that Keaton was not just a faded face from the crackly silent era, but a man still capable of a lot, even in his sixties. As evident in the likes of The Railrodder, Keaton was still highly able to carry a picture, was as physically fit as an elderly man could be, and was as funny as ever before. Still, it is rather ironic that these bit parts were the Buster films most people in this era were seeing.

In 1964, Buster signed up to American International Pictures for four films, none of which really used him to his full abilities. The first of these was 1964's Pyjama Party, in which Keaton appears dressed as a Native American, shouting out "Kowabunga" at random. It was hardly Sherlock Jr. That said, he does have a good perfume fight with a young girl in, one of the film's (very) few highlights.

In 1965 he popped up in some more dated pictures. How to Stuff A Wild Bikini has Keaton featured in separate scenes as a witch doctor, but he looks desperately bored, even if he is being as professional as he can in such dire proceedings. According to some reports and cast accounts, Buster was not enjoying himself, and appeared down beat between takes. His co star Irene Tsu later admitted she did not know who Buster was at the time, and that he was "weird looking with glass ball eyes. He appeared drunk or just plain ancient." She also recalled his "angry mutterings." Anyone who has seen these pictures will understand why Keaton might have felt grumpy. Once a rival of Chaplin's, reduced to this.

Director of the awful each Beach Blanket Bingo may have given Keaton little to do, but was a long time fan happy to work with an old favourite. "I always loved Buster Keaton. I thought," said William Asher, "what a wonderful person to look on and react to these young kids and to view them as the audience might, to shake his head at their crazy antics. He loved it. He would bring me bits and routines. He'd say, 'How about this?' and it would just be this wonderful, inventive stuff. A lot of the audience seemed to be seeing Buster for the first time. Once the kids in the cast became aware of who he was, they all respected him and were crazy about him. And the other comics who came in—Paul Lynde, Don Rickles, Buddy Hackett—they hit it off with him great."

If the younger cast members really did gather round Buster in the filming breaks, and delight in his anecdotes of the silent era, it was a shame that younger viewers would not be enjoying Buster at his best. The poor scripts didn't leave much room for him, and he comes across as bumblingly clumsy in these pictures.

Buster's next big screen bit part was in Richard Lester's popular A Funny Thing Happened On the Way to the Forum. Filmed in 1965, it wasn't released until 1966, after Keaton's death, becoming his final posthumous curtain call. Much better than the lesser feature films he had done the previous two years, it was a fitting part for a legend, directed by a master of the screen, who had already wowed the world with his Beatles movies (Help and A Hard Day's Night) and work with Spike Milligan. American born, UK based Lester went on to have a remarkable career after the film, and obviously cherished working with Keaton. Buster also seems to have been a major influence. "In numerous interviews," wrote FSR in an insightful, if probing article on Lester's pictures. "Richard Lester has listed Buster Keaton as a formative influence in his career, not only in terms of comedy but towards his cinematic education more broadly. Keaton had a keen and intuitive sense of comedy as a form of spectacle, but furthermore was also interested in the mechanics of filmmaking itself - how a sense of reality is fabricated through cinema's devices, and how to elegantly but defiantly bend those devices in order to dance across the line that structures coherent cinematic logic. And I can't think of a more fitting way to describe Lester's similarly rich and inventive contributions to filmmaking than likening them to Keaton's."

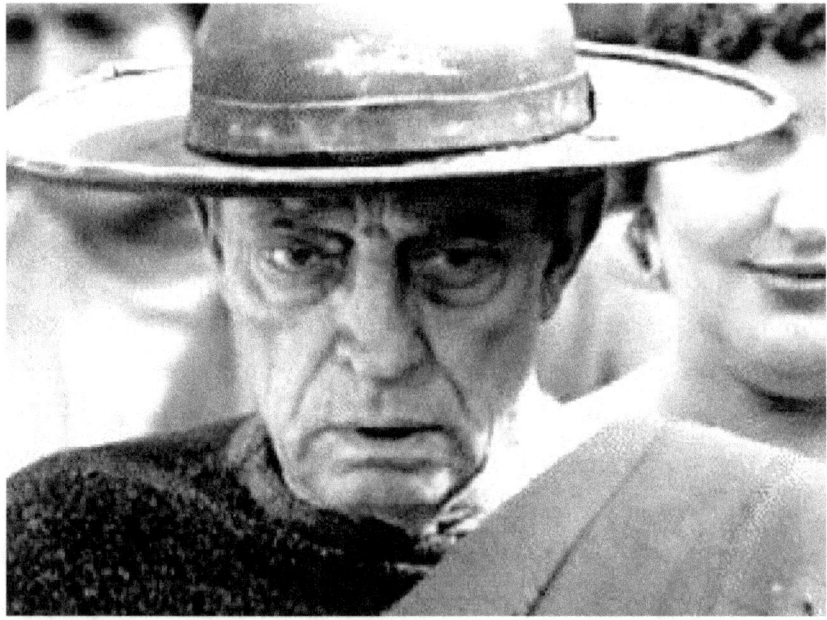

Lester's use of Keaton is much more substantial than what other directors had been doing with the legend around this time. While many of these blink-and-you'll-miss-them bits were knowing nods to a legend, Lester actually gives Keaton some real screen time, and a very memorable scene where Buster walks straight into a tree; though for once, due to his ill health and age, he used a stuntman.

"He was the first person that enchanted me," Lester later said, "in terms of sitting in the cinema and watching films. I didn't really know what cinema had to offer until I saw Keaton's films. When the opportunity came up to work with him I leapt at it, because he was the master. He was dying, it was a shock. But no one seemed to realise what state he was in."

In retrospect it seems a shame that in his winter years, feature films and major studios couldn't give Keaton a final shot as a lead. While in the independent scene he was given the kind of free reign Hollywood had once granted him, the major movies were mostly humouring him. If he impressed younger viewers enough to get them investigating his classic films though, then it was all worthwhile. Foe me though, Keaton's brief dalliances with the world of 1960s mainstream cinema are the least interesting parts of his final era. Ironically, the New Hollywood boom - arriving in the late sixties with Dennis Hopper leading the way with his seminal masterpiece Easy Rider - the very wave of filmmakers who rebelled against such pictures as Beach Blanket Bingo, were influenced by the brave original auteurs like Keaton, whose fall from grace at the hands of an outdated system inspired their cinematic journeys, and also made it possible for them to indulge themselves at the cost of the studios. The sad thing is that these people did not arrive until after Buster's death, and lord knows what they might have done with the veteran. Just imagine it - Woody Allen and Buster Keaton on screen together. If only he'd lived a decade longer. I can but dream...

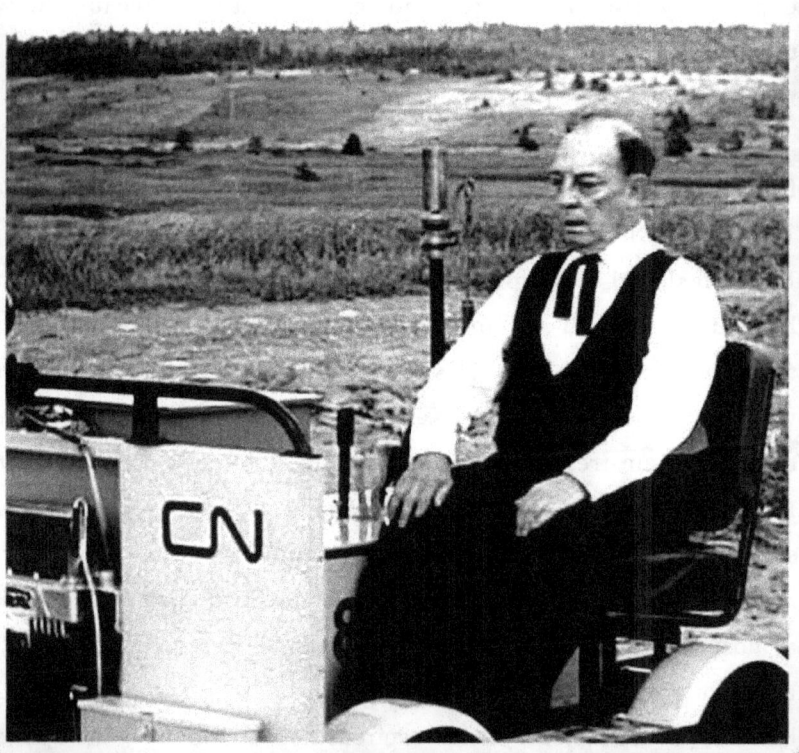

THE
RAILRODDER

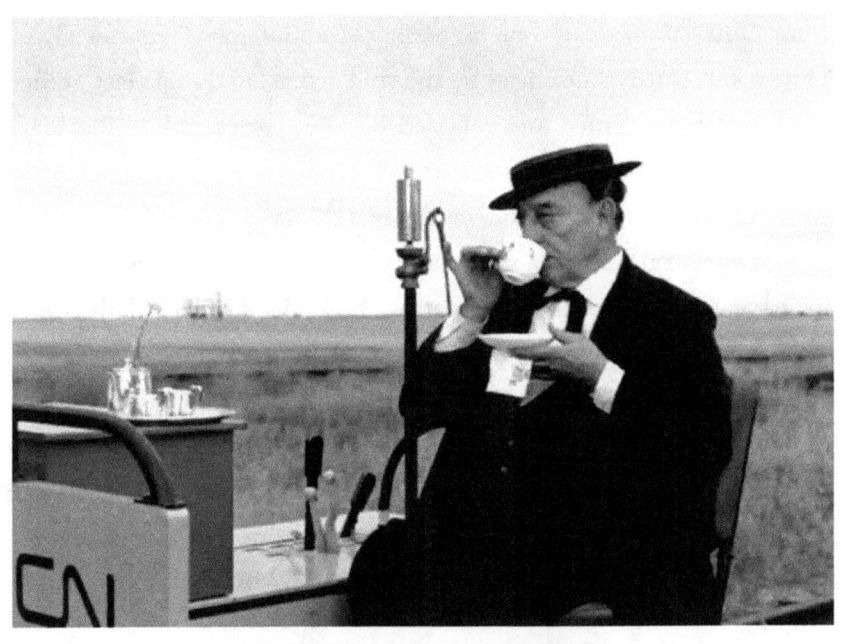

THE RAILRODDER

Buster Keaton, Gerald Potterton and the Swan Song of a Silent Movie Legend

There seems to be no better place to start than here when trying to convince someone that Keaton was not a spent force in his elder years, arguably the last truly great film Buster Keaton starred in. Few screen legends in the history of cinema, especially ones who endured a slip in popularity and status, finished their careers with a movie that could measure up to the classics of their glory years. Chaplin did it with 1952's Limelight (featuring Buster himself in a supporting role) but it was completed 25 years before his death. Other stars of the silent era, such as Roscoe Arbuckle, Clara Bow and Mary Pickford, were either long dead, out of work, or completely forgotten. Even Laurel and Hardy were dead by the mid sixties, and their last golden work had been filmed and released decades earlier, while the Marx Brothers had long disbanded, though Groucho was admittedly still enjoying a healthy TV and celebrity life style. Harold Lloyd had retired years earlier too, a rich man living off the money he earned in his heyday, but unwilling for theatres or TV to show his old movies.

Buster Keaton however, had come back in a cultish way bordering on the highly unexpected. He had regained his popularity, especially in Europe, where his films enjoyed fresh screenings to new, open minded audiences, and on American TV he had been embraced as a comic genius ideal for this rising new medium. No one was more surprised than Buster himself, who was in disbelief at this turn around.

Come 1965, only a year before his death, he starred in one of his finest two-reeler comedies, The Railrodder, produced by Canada's National Board and directed by an English filmmaker called Gerald Potteron. The Railrodder remains fantastic today, over fifty years on, as does the revealing hour-long documentary, Buster Keaton Rides Again, released shortly after, which charts the filming and completion of Potterton's short comedy.

Released in October of 1965, The Railrodder won praise at the Berlin Film Festival, and proved to be one of Keaton's final parts. He died only a matter of months later in February of the following year. It proved to be a fitting swan song for the great man, going out on top in a film that both recalled his early glories and gave a knowing nod to them.

That said, The Railrodder is much more than a tribute to a golden era. It is in fact a highly imaginative trip across Canada, and a glimpse into the restless comic mind of Buster Keaton. It goes right to the centre of the hearts of all serious film lovers the world over. Anyone who ever got a thrill out of Buster Keaton risking his life on the railroad tracks in the silent era will no doubt be on board this crazy train for sure.

Getting in touch with Gerald Potterton was something of a thrill in itself. I love the work he did with Buster. Most Keaton and silent comedy fans will wax lyrical over The General, The Navigator, Seven Chances, his classic early shorts like One Week and The Scarecrow, not to mention now celebrated features like Steamboat Bill Jr. and Sherlock Jr.; and rightly so, for in my view they were rarely matched, never mind bettered, in their time, or since. There is a truth to Keaton's classic work, an openness and an honesty, as well as a surreal magic that was absent from the work of most of his contemporaries. But The Railrodder is right up there too, a touching return to form, with Keaton riding high again, living life on the edge for the sake of our collective entertainment.

I asked Gerald Potterton, a film veteran himself, all about working with Keaton, and he was gracious enough to wind back the clock and think again of that legendary icon.

How did you come to be involved in the film?

I was going to work at the National Film Board one morning and noticed a railroad guy zip across an over pass on a motorized track car. As I was looking for an idea to produce a short animated travel film and had always loved railways, I thought seeing Canada from one of those little carts might be worth looking into. Someone at work suggested I shoot the film in live action and then Buster's name came up.

Were you excited to be working with Keaton?

Of course, since I was a kid and often watched him on Saturday morning movies at the Odeon Clapham. He was a kind of humorous God to me.

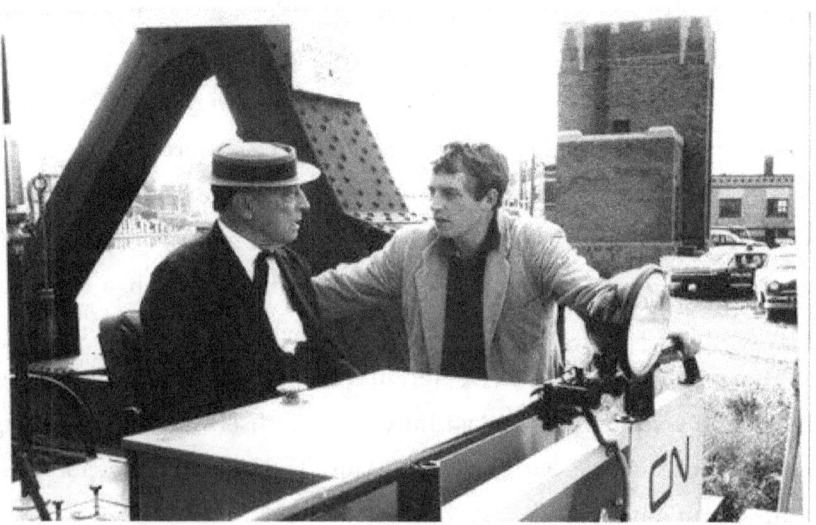

Do you recall your first meeting with him?

It was in his hotel room overlooking Central Park. He was staying there with his wife Eleanor while working on a short experimental film based on an idea by Becket. The traffic noise outside was very loud and he went to a wide-open window and yelled out QUIET. I loved that.

The Rairodder is simply wonderful, one of my favourite Buster movies actually. Was it a kind of pinch-yourself experience working with one of the true legends of silent comedy?

Thanks for the compliment. On the first day of shooting I remember thinking, "I haven't a clue how I'm gonna get through this"... Fortunately for me Buster was a dream to work with and we just got on with it....

I love the fact you had a healthy collaborative relationship together. Were you surprised by the way you could both be open and honest about decisions in the film?

Except for that folding map gag over that long trestle bridge, we never really disagreed about anything. Fortunately I can draw and storyboard a gag situation which I think he appreciated. Him shooting into a tunnel just as he was firing at wild ducks was storyboarded for example, but it was Buster's idea to build and hide in that little duck blind. It made the gag much richer.

During the making of the film, there is a very moving part where he is presented a birthday cake and looks terribly shy. Did you find him a warm person when the cameras were off?

Off camera Buster was a busy, sociable guy who laughed and talked his head off. Never a dull moment. He seemed to really love people and despite some really bad personal years he loved life and certainly loved his wife Eleanor who shared his sociable personality.

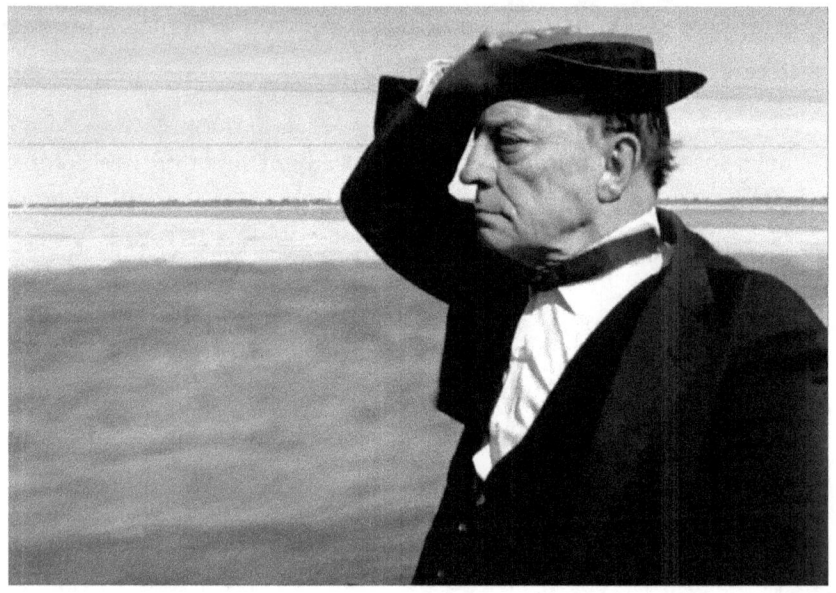

What are some of your favourite moments from the filming?

We shot the film in sequence from Canada's East Coast to the West and were entirely at the mercy of the railroads schedules and limited time and changing weather, so it was exhausting for me at least, and quite a few others on the crew. There weren't many of us but generally we were a happy little crowd and knew we were onto something rare and interesting to work on. Buster's birthday party was a great memory for me, and shooting through the Rockies and down the great Fraser River was also very special.

What did Buster think of the finished film?

He said..."Bootiful photography."

I love the wide mix of work you have done, but working with Keaton must surely be one of the things you are most proud of.

You got that right mate.

Are you glad to see he gets his credit now and that your film is part of that rich legacy?

Chris, it gives me nothing but pleasure. Buster was the real Mc Coy in every way. Spending time with Buster was a treat and as a long ago nitwit from Balham I was extremely lucky to get to know and work with him.

The film begins with Keaton in London, the opening shot of Big Ben establishing this in the first second. The camera pans down over London Bridge, where Keaton sits (obviously in a studio with London on a screen behind him) reading a newspaper. Opening it up, it says in large letters, SEE CANADA NOW. Keaton breaks the fourth wall instantly and looks to the camera. It's a light bulb moment. He will go to Canada, and he will go there now!

American imagery flashes through his head, as red buses and black cars whizz behind him. Buster folds up his newspaper, climbs on to the side of London bridge and jumps off into the water. In the next scene he is emerging from the sea on to the beach, and after looking around sees that he has gone in the right direction. After realising that his desired location is almost 4000 miles away, Keaton starts to walk the train line, bumbling along the tracks in classic Keaton style. He stumbles upon a track speeder and shiftily sits on it. When it takes suddenly off, Buster is instantly speeding down the rail line holding on for dear life. A few seconds in though, despite the speed, he realises it's actually rather relaxing. Better still, there's a box at the front with a jacket to warm him up, and, you guessed it, a brand new flat hat, which he places on his head, given that his own was lost in the sea. His dazzling journey begins, this gleeful rail trip across Canada, narrowly missing oncoming trains (knowing nods to his classic work) and zig zagging cars.

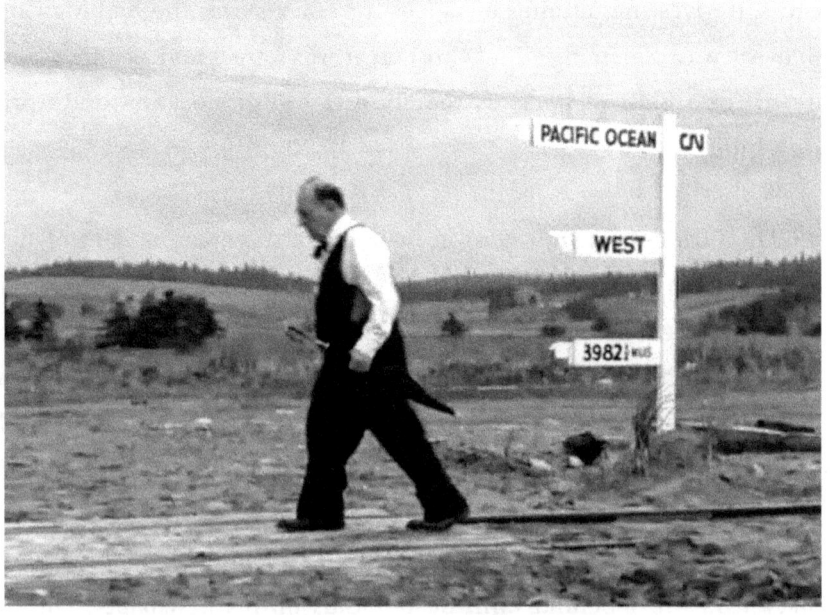

As a love letter to Canada, The Railrodder does the trick, and as a tribute to a legend, it doesn't really get any better, seeing as though the legend himself is actually present. In his late sixties, Buster impresses with his sheer daring, standing on the speeder at points and looking like he has no care in the world.

Things get complex for Buster when the speeder breaks down on a bridge, which opens up to make room for a passing boat just as he finds himself stuck on it. Oblivious to the fact, Keaton hunches over and fixes the speeder, which gets back on its way the very second the bridge returns to its normal position. A little touch of Buster genius.

To frantic banjo music, Keaton's journey goes on, through tunnels, across country side and past huge factories. Beautifully shot (Buster was right when he commented on the cinematography for sure), the film is a feast for the eyes as well as a comforting ride down memory lane with your favourite silent star.

The next day, Buster is still on the speeder, and he freshens up as he would if he were at home for the busy hours ahead. After all, it's going to be a long ride. Buster begins to find the speeder more relaxing, reading a paper and reclining, while he only seems scared when a passing train honks its deafening horn at him. Through the mountains and thick forests, Buster does a nice routine where he sits and has a meal, before he gets a bit tired, finds a blanket and has a little nap.

When he awakes, he finds the speeder has stopped on the track in the middle of nowhere. He gets it running again and continues in his journey, doing a very dangerous routine involving the map covering his face while standing up on the speeder. Like a human Bugs Bunny cartoon, Buster defies all logic and pulls the stunts off wonderfully. Various shots and images stick in the mind, like the close up of Buster holding his hat on his head in the high wind, dozing off again and snoring despite the frantic speed he is travelling. Rather than being hilarious, it comes across as beautiful, poignant and often rather moving.

That said there are little scenes here which measure up to his old days. The posh English tea break is a nice touch, with Buster even upping the pinky finger like a proper reserved gent. Donning a head scarf, Buster gets out the duster and broom and gives his speeder home a clean over. There is also a brilliant bit involving an old camera, which Buster fails to operate due to the force of the wind.

Potterton excels in his shooting, getting some breathtaking views in as he follows Buster. The mountains are stunning, and the Canadian board must have been pleased how the film endorsed their great and beautiful nation.

One of my favourite bits is when Buster dons his huge fur coat and decides to do a spot of knitting (he wore a similar coat in the Lester Snapwell film, maybe even the same one), one of the most surreal and plain odd sequences in the movie. Buster is later startled by a flock of birds, and tries to hide from them in various dangerous ways, firstly behind the side of the speeder, then by trying to get inside the box. Neither work, so Buster stops the speeder and cuts down some trees, putting them around him as camouflage on the speeder and arming himself with a gun. It's a bizarre and brilliant scene, one of the film's laugh out loud moments of unexpected glee. Typical for Keaton, he manages to get a deck of cards in (Keaton was a famous card player), adding another subtle personal touch.

Twenty minutes in and the film is winding down. It goes by so fast that 20 minutes just hasn't felt like enough (an hour might have been more suitable, though perhaps thinking up new ideas for 60 minutes might have been too challenging for Buster and Potterton), but Keaton is nearly at the end of the line. Cooking himself a nice fried egg (even flipping it in the pan), he enjoys his hot meal before realising he has reached the Pacific Ocean. Turning the speeder around and stopping it, Buster gets out and takes in his surroundings. Oddly, a Chinese man dressed in the same outfit as Buster arrives from the water and comes towards the camera. Glancing at the sign, he wishes to head in the opposite direction, East. When Buster's back is turned, while he stares dreamily out at the sea, the Asian Buster takes the speeder and belts off. Buster, with a calm shrug, accepts the situation and begins to walk down the track. The film ends and the credits roll.

In my view, many write ups of The Railrodder seem to have misunderstood its aim and point. While some may argue it is not that funny, Buster's comedy was always about keeping a few elements in balance, and only one of them was humour. Though he often chased the big laughs, he also wanted to create beauty on the screen, and was obsessed with the technical side. For instance, Sherlock Jr. is hardly laugh out loud hilarious, but its use of early special effects and surreal imagery make it a spellbinding and impressive feat. Even The General was not constantly funny, instead a dazzling series of life endangering stunts and cinematic thrills. The Railrodder may not have you rolling on the floor, but it will give you a warm feeling, make you smile, and please certain aspects of your film viewing hunger. It is also very poignant.

The AV Club, who so often seem to misunderstand the ageing Buster, had this to say about The Railrodder and his status at the time of it making. "In 1964, Buster Keaton's languishing career was experiencing a sort of semi-renaissance. Critics were rediscovering and wildly praising his great silent comedies of the '20s, and offers of movie and television roles were flooding in. But by and large, Keaton was popularly regarded as a quaint relic of Hollywood's distant past; he was never given anything larger than a cameo or supporting part, and certainly little that suited his deadpan, stoic, slightly surreal comic persona. The National Film Board of Canada attempted to rectify this by casting the nearly 70-year-old Keaton in The Railrodder, a short film depicting his travels across the Canadian landscape on a motorized handcar. Despite the laudable attempt to evoke Keaton's early work in two-reelers - as well as his thematic preoccupation with the fickle nature of machines - The Railrodder does not quite succeed as comedy, mainly due to the mildness of the gags and a paltry storyline."

The success of the Railrodder, quite simply, depends on how big a fan you are of Buster Keaton. Anyone with a fondness for the man and his unique skills would find it hard not to be entertained and charmed, and if you take it on the grounds of what it truly is, a final goodbye from one of the silver screen's finest comic performers, then you will come away pleased. Even a non-fan might enjoy it for the scenery alone. On The Silver Screenings website, the writer goes for the view that the scenery might just be too beautiful and detract from the star at the forefront. "Canada looks beautiful and majestic and interesting," they write. "Which creates an unusual dilemma. Keaton is billed as the star of the show, and rightfully so. He's funny, engaging and utterly entertaining. But he has to work to steal the scene from the main character: Canada. In our opinion some of the most impressive Canadian scenery is left out of the film. Yet, the varied landscapes – from ocean to prairie to mountain – make you appreciate how big this place is. (Canada is the second largest nation, area-wise, in the world.) There's absolutely no one else besides Buster Keaton you'd want riding a speeder across Canada. But when he's in the Rockies, for instance, you hardly notice him. The mountains look so crisp and inviting it's easy to get lost in the scenery."

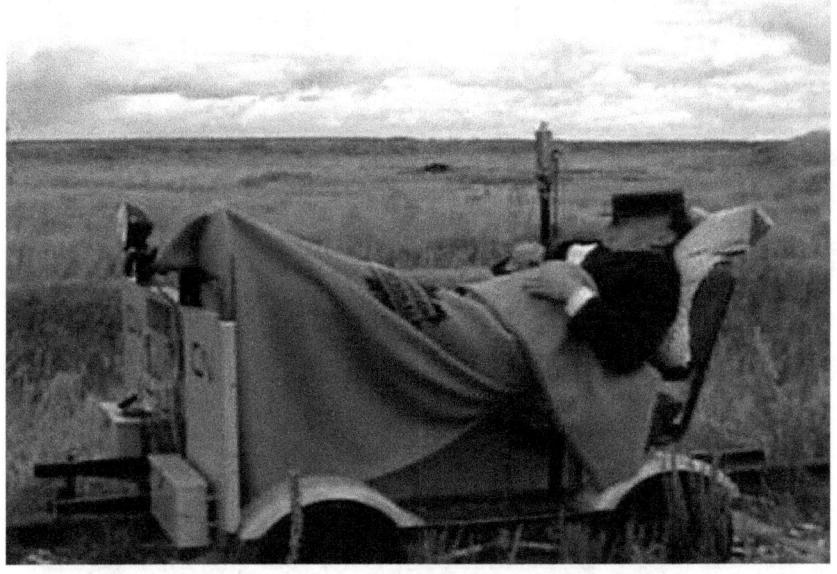

Even though he is 69 in the film, Keaton doesn't go easy on himself, not does he show any real sign of age. The General, filmed 40 years earlier, may have been more explosive, extravagant and cinematically grandiose, but there is something in the low key, much more modest Railrodder which feels more honest and real. Buster, dying at the time, bookends his own career without realising it, sealing off a rich legacy with this addictive, endlessly re-watchable little gem.

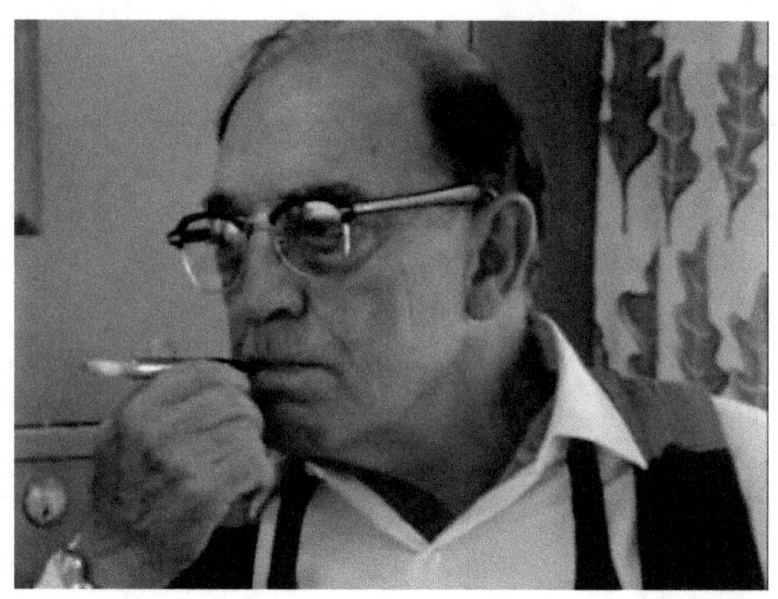

BUSTER KEATON RIDES AGAIN

Inside the Documentary

POTTERTON: "That's the whole centre of the gag,
is that long shot of the bridge."
KEATON: "Oh, no, the bridge is not your gag, the bridge is
only suspense - a thrill. There's no gag to the bridge at all,
doesn't mean a goddamn thing."

There are numerous documentaries on the life and career of Buster
Keaton, some more revealing and absorbing than others. As far as
career retrospectives go, one cannot ask for more than Kevin
Brownlow's three part series, Buster Keaton: A Hard Act to Follow,
which features interviews with Eleanor Keaton, as well as many

collaborators, directors and friends. It's an excellent portrait of a genius. Other films, such as The Real Buster Keaton and The Genius Crushed By Hollywood are also good, but the latter is rather depressing. However, one documentary just might out do them all. While making the excellent Railroader film with Gerald Potterton in 1965, a crew led by director John Spotton charted the filming and got up close access to Keaton's process. The only close up footage showing Keaton getting down on set (save for some amateur footage of the New York location shoot of The Cameraman), it's an invaluable glimpse into Buster's inner workings and endless creativity on the set - or in this case, on location.

First off, Buster Keaton Rides Again runs for 55 minutes, and since The Railrodder itself only ran for 25, the documentary is actually double the length of the film of which it charts the creation. Again funded by the National Film Board of Canada, the film proved to capture Buster in his final months, offering wisdom, telling tales, and perhaps most touching of all, celebrating his 69th birthday. As a complete glimpse into Buster's way of working, nothing could hope to come close.

Filmed in black and white, the film also cleverly looks into Keaton's illustrious past while contrasting it to the present day. It begins with a powerful bang, an image of Keaton putting on his oversized shoes. While he ties his laces, he informs us in his rich, gravely voice, that he's a size 7 but wearing elevens. As Potterton, the crew and Buster prepare for their next scene, the narrator begins to chart the life of this living legend. He informs us that "the last 35 years have been a bit rocky," in what has to be the biggest understatement of all time. He adds, quietly, "Buster is still doing business." He was in fact doing much more than that. Vital and active on the set, he and Potterton are clearly impassioned by every detail of the film, and far from being an ageing comic taking an easy pay cheque, Keaton is in the thick of it, offering ideas, taking intense interest in proceedings and, as becomes clear, coming up with fresh gags all of his own. Though Potterton is credited as director and writer, Keaton is clearly responsible for some of the gold.

One of the first scenes involves Keaton and Potterton discussing whether that rail worker would run after Buster or not after he steals the speeder, or throw off his hat. Keaton is adamant the man should not be required to act. As Potterton and Keaton stand around, Buster begins to recall the early days of Hollywood, and the film then whizzes back to 1915 with the arrival of cinema's popularity. Cue lots of silent movie scenes, old stills and a brief reeling off of all the popular stars. The film explains how Buster rose from vaudeville frolics to film stardom. It also goes through the difficult period, when Buster became a boozer, lost his house and lost his family. Thankfully, it does not dwell on the negative aspects too long, and zooms right back to 1965, celebrating the fact that Keaton was now free to make films once again, despite a down turn in the thirties and forties, and his struggles to make it in the talkie era.

While filming The Railrodder, Keaton has the crew cracking up, and we see his interactions with his beloved wife Eleanor. In his private train carriage, the camera gets to see how Buster spent his down time on set. Playing the ukelele while his wife keeps affairs in order, Buster comes across as rather child like, in a charming way, and Eleanor seems almost motherly to him. Very heart warming.

In the streets of Canada, Keaton wanders the malls and stores, meeting fans, shaking hands, signing autographs and goofing around with his admirers. It's a charming segment of the film, and shows just how Keaton's star was once again on the rise, and how much people truly adored him and his work.

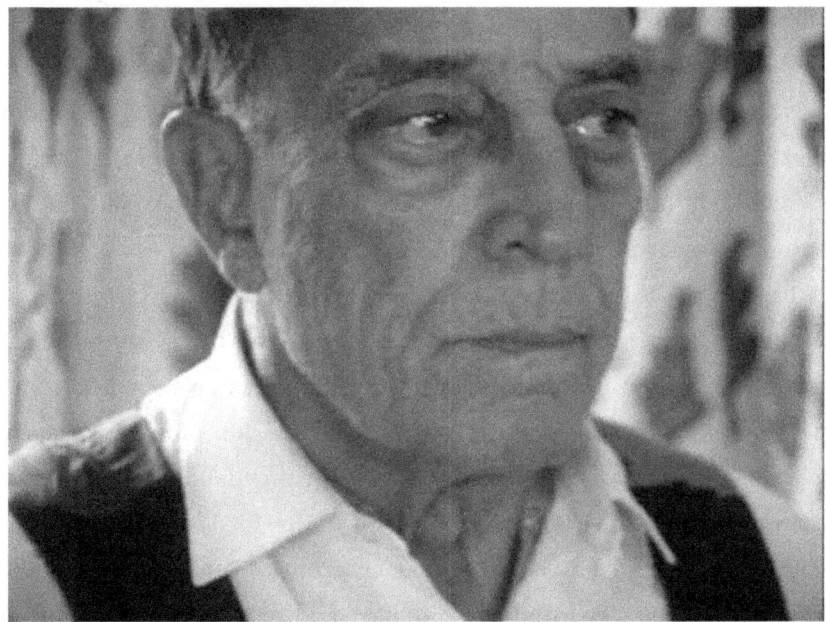

The best scenes for me though, come when Keaton is out there filming, doing little gags and pranks to pass the time. My favourite part in fact is only a few seconds long. It involves Buster making it look like he's stopped the train with one hand, and then when it takes off again, as if he has pulled it back into action. He seems light hearted, fun, funny and warm to everyone on set. Clearly, he is enjoying himself making The Railrodder, mainly because he is not just being asked to goof around for a single scene and then leave the set, but be a vital part of the production. He and Potterton bounce ideas around, agree and disagree on small considerations, but on the whole make a great partnership. Potterton is clearly worried at points, but Buster eases any unsettling thoughts with his earthy charm. Two very different men (one an ageing American film star, the other a young English filmmaker) getting along in order to make the best film they can with their collective powers.

One of the best parts is when Buster entertains the crew in his carriage with tales of the old days in Hollywood, revealing secrets of how those gems were made. When the dead duck arrives, Buster is clearly delighted. Hilariously, it was written in his contract that he should have a wild duck dinner.

Back in the thick of the filming, Keaton is something of a force of nature, pulling ideas together as if directing the thing himself. The fact that Potterton includes him in decision making says a lot, and perhaps explains why the film is so good. Potterton himself is clearly a great director, but having Keaton as a direct collaborator can't have done any harm. Keaton hadn't directed a film for years, but still has what it takes and has not lost that charming dictatorial command. He has that instinct to be a filmmaker, and even becomes stubborn over certain decisions that he disagrees with. Told that he can't do a particularly dangerous gag, Keaton says "I've done more dangerous stuff in my sleep. It's child's play..." Keaton's persistence paid off - the gag ended up in the film.

There are other wonderful scenes too, like when Buster receives an honour at a lavish function, and when the crew lovingly present him with his birthday cake. There is another glimpse into his hatred of crowds, or his discomfort with them at least, when he finds himself overwhelmed by the gang of reporters probing him and flashing

140

their cameras in his face. He sees the press conference as a burden and cannot wait to get out.

Elsewhere though, Keaton is enjoying himself, and the scene in which the children ask if Buster can play is absolutely wonderful, especially when he gets the ukulele out and gives them a song.

Anyone under the impression that Keaton was an unhappy, bitter, faded old comic need only watch Buster Keaton Rides Again. He is a man at the peak of his powers despite being at the end of his life; he is charming, funny and open; people adore him; he is in a happy marriage; and best of all perhaps, he is still brilliant, still Buster and still capable of making movie magic.

Streamline, on their fabulous website, wrote that they were pleasantly surprised upon first viewing the film, expecting a very different atmosphere and picture of the ageing, dying Keaton. "Glancing at only a couple reviews, which seemed to focus on aspects of ill health and a fall from grace," they write, "I couldn't help but feel that watching Buster Keaton Rides Again might make for melancholic viewing. But I'm happy to report that my experience of this film was quite the opposite. True, Keaton is seen at the end of his years with a tell-tale cough, and he also seems accustomed to a modest and earnest lifestyle. But herein lies the key to what made this such a heart-warming document; unlike some VH1 special that chronicles the rise-and-fall of some mega-star, happily lolling around in the slop of the decline like some pig in mud, Buster Keaton Rides Again instead shows us a humble giant, still revelling in his creative impulses and ageing gracefully without a big chip on his shoulder. He's accessible, witty, charming, gracious and, obviously, full of great stories."

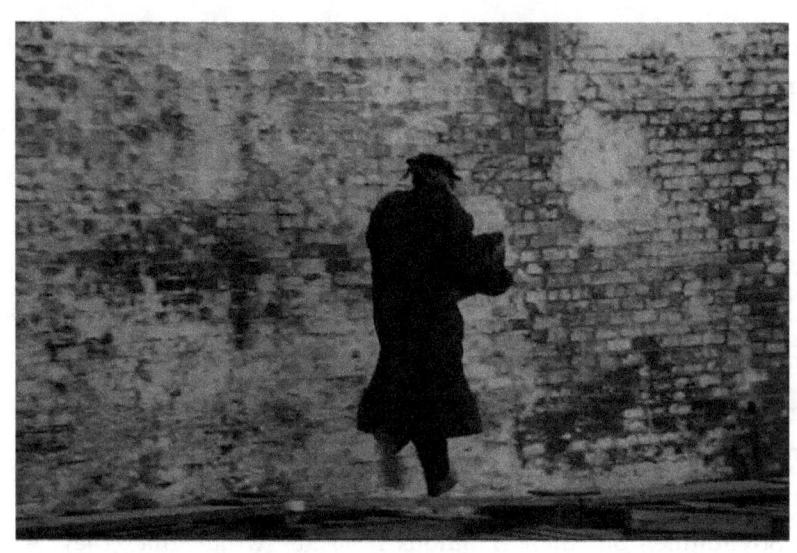

WHEN BECKETT MET KEATON

Buster and the Avant-Garde in "Film"

"The heat was terrible - while I was staggering in the humidity, Keaton was galloping up and down and doing whatever we asked of him. He had great endurance, he was very tough and, yes, reliable. And when you saw that face at the end - oh! He smiled, at last..."
- Samuel Beckett on filming with Buster Keaton

One of the strangest parings of the 1960s just has to be that of Samuel Beckett and Buster Keaton, who collaborated together on the surreal short film, simply titled "Film". The only screenplay penned by the acclaimed playwright, Beckett wrote it in April of 1963, and revised it in May. An enigmatic, mysterious experiment, Beckett wanted director Alan Schneider to help bring it to screen, the man who had been staging acclaimed stage versions of his work for a while. Ironically, it was not Keaton who Beckett had in mind for the part, but Keaton's old friend, Charlie Chaplin. He sent the script along but it is not actually known whether Chaplin read it, or even received it for that matter. Other suggestions for the part of O in the film included Zero Mostel, but it was Schneider who came up with the idea of casting Buster. They flew out to LA to meet with him, offered him a decent pay cheque, and that was that.

Buster had been baffled by Beckett's play, Waiting For Godot, which is ironic, as some say it was based on a Keaton film, The Loveable Cheat, in which Keaton's partner is called Godot. When Schneider got to Keaton and visited him at his home, he was surprised to see him unwell and skint, and "playing cards with invisible Hollywood producers" - obviously a nod to his turn in Sunset Boulevard. People say Keaton accepted the offer flat out, while actor James Karen, who co-stars in the often baffling film, says that his wife Eleanor had to persuade him to take on the part. These conflicting accounts and views offer varied tales, some more interesting than others.

In their early meetings, Beckett recalled Keaton was far from inspiring and hardly even into the project. Perhaps forgetting the fact that Keaton was actually dying before his eyes, he recalled to Kevin Brownlow, "Buster Keaton was inaccessible. He had a poker mind as well as a poker face. I doubt if he ever read the text - I don't think he approved of it or liked it. But he agreed to do it and he was very competent. Of course, I had seen his silent films and enjoyed them – don't suppose I could remember them now. He had a young woman with him – his wife, who had picked him up from his alcoholism. We met him at a hotel. I tried to engage him in conversation, but it was no good. He was absent. He didn't even offer us a drink. Not because he was being unfriendly, but because it never occurred to him."

Schneider says the two men had nothing to say to one another - Beckett and Keaton, two very different men with very different backgrounds and ideas about what film was, is and should be. Just as Keaton found Beckett's ideas pretentious and unreachable, Beckett seemed to relish in belittling Keaton's films to something from his childhood, long forgotten; and when he did see one again (The General as it happens) took great delight in saying how disappointed he was.

During filming, Schneider also said Keaton was nothing but a pro. "Keaton's behaviour on the set was steady and cooperative. He was indefatigable if not exactly loquacious. To all intents and purposes, we were shooting a silent film, and he was in his best form. He encouraged to give him vocal directions during the shot, sometimes starting over again without stopping the camera if he felt he hadn't done something well the first time. (Nor did he believe much in rehearsal, preferring the spontaneity of performance.) Often when the crew was stumped over a technical problem with the camera, he came through with suggestions, inevitably prefacing his comments by explaining that he had solved such problems many times at the Keaton Studios back in 1927."

Schneider also smoothed over the rumours of Keaton's indifference to the film, stating, "Whatever he may have subsequently said to interviewers or reporters about not understanding a moment of what he was doing or what the film was about, what I remember best of our final farewell on the set was that he smiled and half-admitted those six pages were worth doing after all."

As for the finished film, Buster was right. It was definitely worth doing. The intense short is open to much interpretation, and even if the subtext, theories and meanings make your head spin, you can at least enjoy the imagery for how it is presented, and the use of Buster, who is rather oddly faced away from the camera for most of the 24 minutes. Intellectual dissection is not totally essential when enjoying Film; in fact, it's probably more entertaining as a stand alone piece, especially when one doesn't read or get too involved in the Beckett screenplay, which some - perhaps his theatre devotees - would rather see as the definitive article than the film itself.

The film starts with a reveal of an eye lid (shades of Un Chein Andalou), which then opens and reveals the eye in close up. We then follow Buster as O, a man hurriedly making his way across a brick wall. He is holding a suitcase and trying hard not to be seen. We follow O for longer (the camera is referred to, in the script, as E), and he ends up in a corridor. Somehow, despite the shaky camera and very little real action or change, the film is magnetic and pure. Keaton's aging frame becomes increasingly magnetic, his strange movements utterly captivating under Schneider's camera.

O/Buster finally reaches The Room, his goal all along. It's full of various objects and things, and O settles on the rocking chair. After a strange sequence with a folder, O and E come face to face, Buster's front finally up close and personal. He wears an eye patch and stares at E and we the viewer.

Some critics sideline Film as a failed experiment from a writer who knew very little about film, but to toss it aside, I feel, is a big mistake. Yes it may be too clever for its own good, and yes it may waste the legendary face of Keaton, but it utilises his famous frame and provides food for thought, and no doubt stimulating (or boring, depending on your view) conversation between anyone who has taken the time to watch it. Beckett himself called it an interesting failure, but I by no means see it as such. While an experiment can indeed fail, such an individualistic one surely cannot, for it works amidst its own rules. Film is interesting to watch and baffling to consider, which of course is a lethal or fruitful combination, again depending on taste.

"It's a movie about the perceiving eye," Becket later said when asked to summarise the film, rather patronisingly, to the man in the street. He said it was "about the perceived and the perceiver – two aspects of the same man. The perceiver desires like mad to perceive and the perceived tries desperately to hide. Then, in the end, one wins."

Film critic Andrew Sarris hated the film and damned it with this statement: "Even Samuel Beckett contributed to the desecration of the Keaton mask by involving the actor of absurdity before its time in a dreary exercise called Film, the most pretentious title in all cinema."

One will get more rewards if you choose to look at Film, as Sarris indeed did, in the context of Keaton's career rather than its singularity in the Becket filmography. As a man who began his film career nearly fifty years earlier falling about with Roscoe Arbuckle in a butcher's shop, there was something remarkable about seeing

146

Buster as a man, as Buster himself saw the character, who can get away from everyone else but himself. Was there a bit more of Keaton in there than one might think? After all, most of Keaton's work involved him moving, walking, running or travelling. What was he fleeing? Himself? Perhaps so.

In the great arc of Keaton's career, Film sits alongside The Railrodder as one of the last fascinating things he did on the screen. While The Railrodder mirrored and paid homage to the glory years, Film was in an entirely different world. It was the first and last performance and film of its kind. In many ways, one could get frustrated at the thought of not seeing Buster explore other areas of his own performance prism, for he was clearly capable of many varied styles. But in the end, one needs to feel grateful for what he did put on to the screen, and the purely odd ball paring of these two giants.

Though Beckett and Keaton were a world apart, and maybe Keaton didn't quite get it, but Beckett had to admit the legendary clown knew what he was doing. "His movement was excellent - covering up the mirror, putting out the animals - all that was very well done. To cover the mirror, he took his big coat off and he asked me what he was wearing underneath. I hadn't thought of that. I said the same coat... He liked that. The only gag he approved of was the scene where he tries to get rid of the animals - he put out the cat and the dog comes back and he puts out the dog and the cat comes back - that was really the only scene he enjoyed doing."

"What's the film about?" Keaton said. "Well, I'm not too sure myself." And that says it all, that it really doesn't matter.

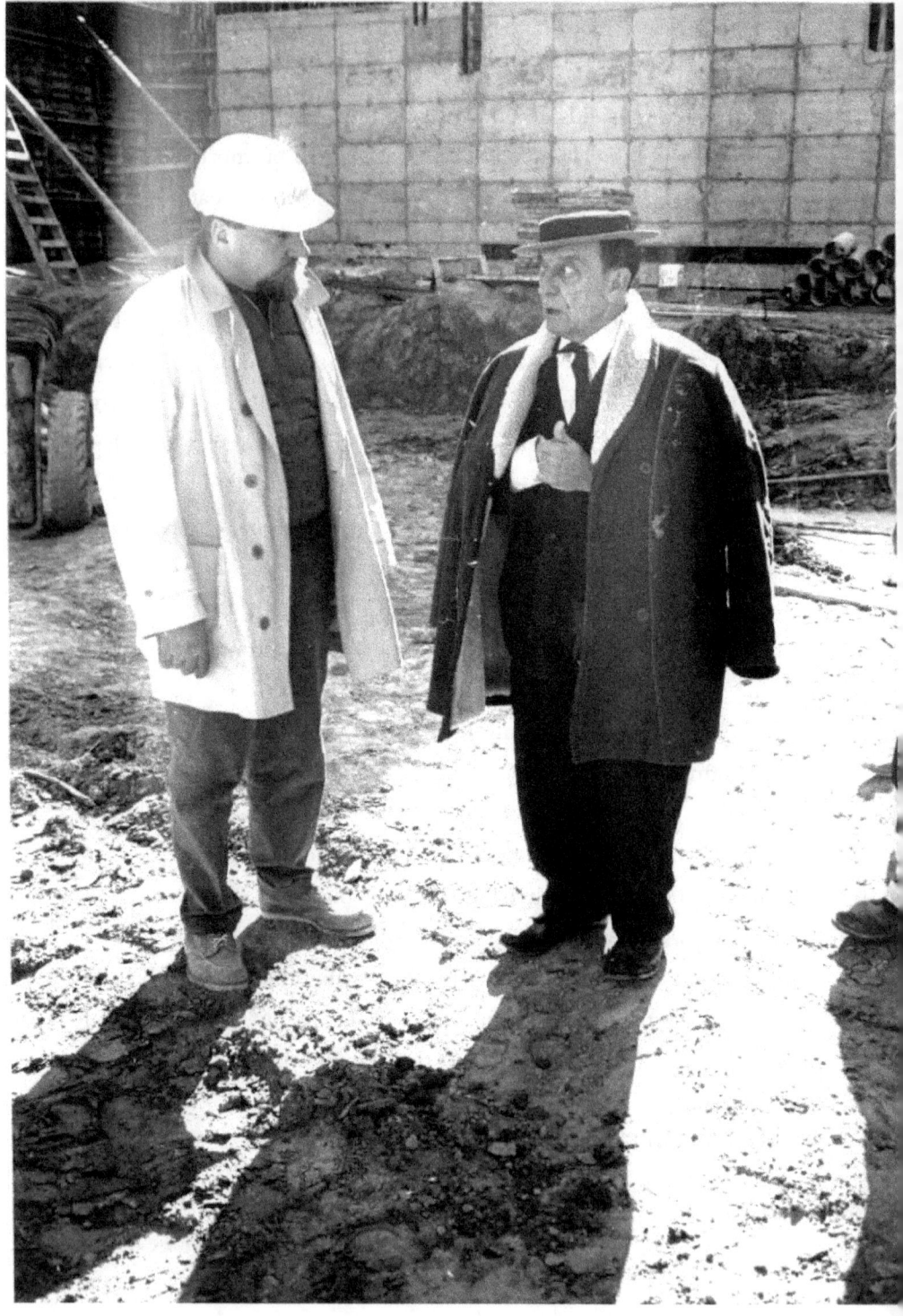

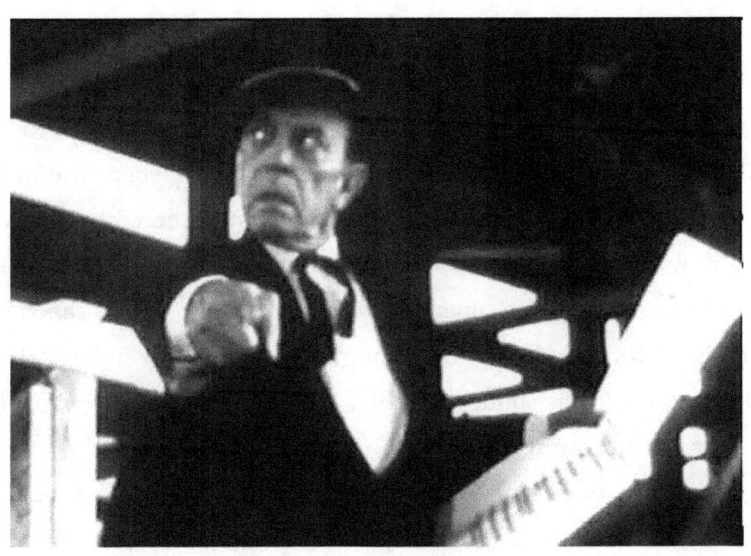

THE SCRIBE

Buster Keaton's Last Dance

Though in his later years, and indeed his final months, Keaton was only getting feature film roles that were blink or you'll miss 'em cameos, he was still contributing to some worthwhile shorts. And in many ways, these mini movies, avant-garde experiments and, in the case of The Scribe, industrial films, were actually closer in both style and length to what he was doing back in the early 20s, in his early two-reelers, and then of course stylistically near his six and seven reel masterpieces. That he was able to soldier on, live modestly in a nice, not over sized home with Eleanor, and still work even as his body was riddled with cancer, is a credit to Keaton's strength. Let's face it, he was built strong,

Having worked in Canada for the excellent Railrodder, Keaton was employed by the Canadians once again, specifically the Construction Safety Association of Ontario, who cast him in their 30 minute safety film, The Scribe. Directed by John Sebert, the quickie features Keaton as a janitor who ends up being ordered by the editor of a newspaper to cover a story about health and safety at a huge construction site. The opening scenes paint a rather harrowing portrait of 1960s industry and though it is merely an industrial film, Sebert's direction is solid, with shots lingering for much longer than a lesser director would have them.

The editor makes his way to work. He sits down at his desk and dials for O'Mally, then goes and peers through the blinds of his office window at the buildings outside. When the journo arrives, the editor reels off the various injuries on construction sites, and deems the casualties news worthy. O'Mally declines the offer and says to let the new guy take the story. The "new guy" just happens to leave the office, and asks Buster, in his usual trademark hat, to take his calls. His first scene involves him cleaning the floor, then struggling to answer the phone properly (there's a lovely muffled voice effect in this section), bumbling round the office in the way only Buster could. Then, having heard enough of the call to get the brief, Buster dons his coat, the farcical music begins, and our hero is on his way.

Buster stands in the middle of a busy road and heads into the site. His ageing face is full of expression, unusually so given that he barely has to even move his features at all. Reading the massive list of safety instructions, we are reminded why this film was financed in the first place - to brief people on safety in the workplace. The boring stuff out of the way, Buster heads outside and immediately gets ejected from the site for not having a hard hat on, and for being a member of the press. Finding a hard hat of his own, he heads back inside, clownishly stumbling across various dangerous set ups. Buster taps a man's hat, who happens to be bending down the improper way. A voice over tells us to avoid improper posture, so Keaton demonstrates the correct way, to bend the knees rather than the back, but ends up falling down flat. He then saves a man from an approaching digger, but he gets his foot caught in a paint tin. Buster ends up being elevated on the digger, and continues on his way, as the narrator warns us of the pitfalls of a busy construction site.

Buster really doesn't have a great deal to do here, but his minimal movements are utilised to their highest potential. If anyone else had done the video, any viewer might have switched off after two minutes; but Keaton's charm keeps you hooked, even though the instructions (always wear your safety boots for instance) are painfully (quite literally in this case) obvious.

The best part for me is when Buster ends up on the metal beams, reading from his oversized safety instruction list while informing the workers where they are going wrong. Buster ends up falling down a hole, and while stuck there refers to his list - "make sure all areas are properly guarded", advises out narrator. Watching Keaton clown around on the ladder and the wooden planks, then dash across the heaps of earth, makes the commitment to a full viewing worth the time.

Though not artful, the camera is as inventive as it can be, and one cannot help but get a thrill from seeing Keaton in such a stark, cold setting. This master of mechanism had shone on the rail tracks, the grind of the engines and smoke only enhancing his strange, almost

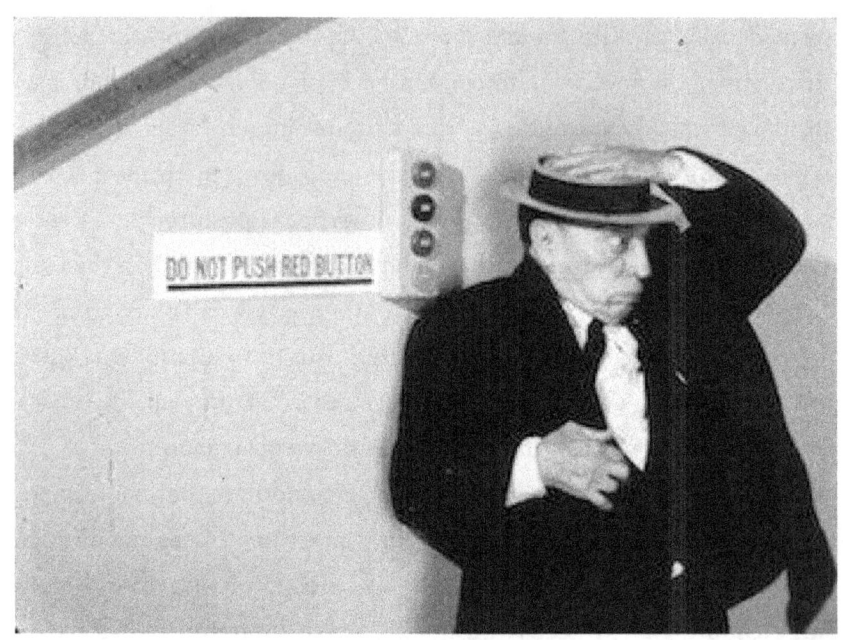

otherworldly features and body. He had always relished exploring the battle of man against machine, of his own inadequacies with technology, and he was at his best when fighting with machinery. Here, nearing the end of his life, the clattering sounds, smoke and heavy grinding produce a similar effect, and Keaton, aged and very close to the end of his life, is brought alive once again by the industrial surroundings. Though this is hardly a great final acting credit (I prefer to view The Railrodder as his true swan song, the film to end his illustrious filmography on), one can only admire Keaton and the fact that he made a 3 minute safety warning video hugely entertaining. He even recreates the mopping scene from 1918's The Bell Boy. Anyway, it's well worth watching until the end, with Buster taking his "article" to the editor (his cough and daft attempts to try and get the boss's attention are mini comic gold), and returning to his room, removing his coat and cleaning the floor once again. It's a lovely ending, the final scene Buster performed.

Though Buster was baffled by the "failed" Beckett experiment, he would more than likely have found the straight forward step by step mechanics of The Scribe more conducive to his slapstick style. Given brief instructions, Buster gets by with subtle movements, surprisingly fit for a man who was not only 70, but also dying of cancer. In many ways, it *is* a great performance, though perhaps not consciously, as some kind of illusion, a man unaware of an impending death, and making us unaware of it too. Keaton is doing exactly what is expected of him, even if the film is a by the numbers safety picture. Still, Sebert ensures his curtain call is a subtle homage to that rich and influential career.

Upon its re-release in 2013, the director himself recalled working with Keaton. "We flew to San Francisco to meet with him and set everything up. When we got there, he said: 'My wife doesn't want me to do it, but I really want to do it.' Whoever granted us permission must've been a Buster fan, because they made it very easy for us to shoot in this location. I still have my reservations about the film. It could be a lot better, but over the years, all sorts of people have wanted to look at it."

Unpretentious, unfussy and pure Buster, The Scribe may not be the accomplished comedy classic The Railrodder so clearly is, but as a last effort, Keaton had gone out in style. Just make sure you remember those safety tips!

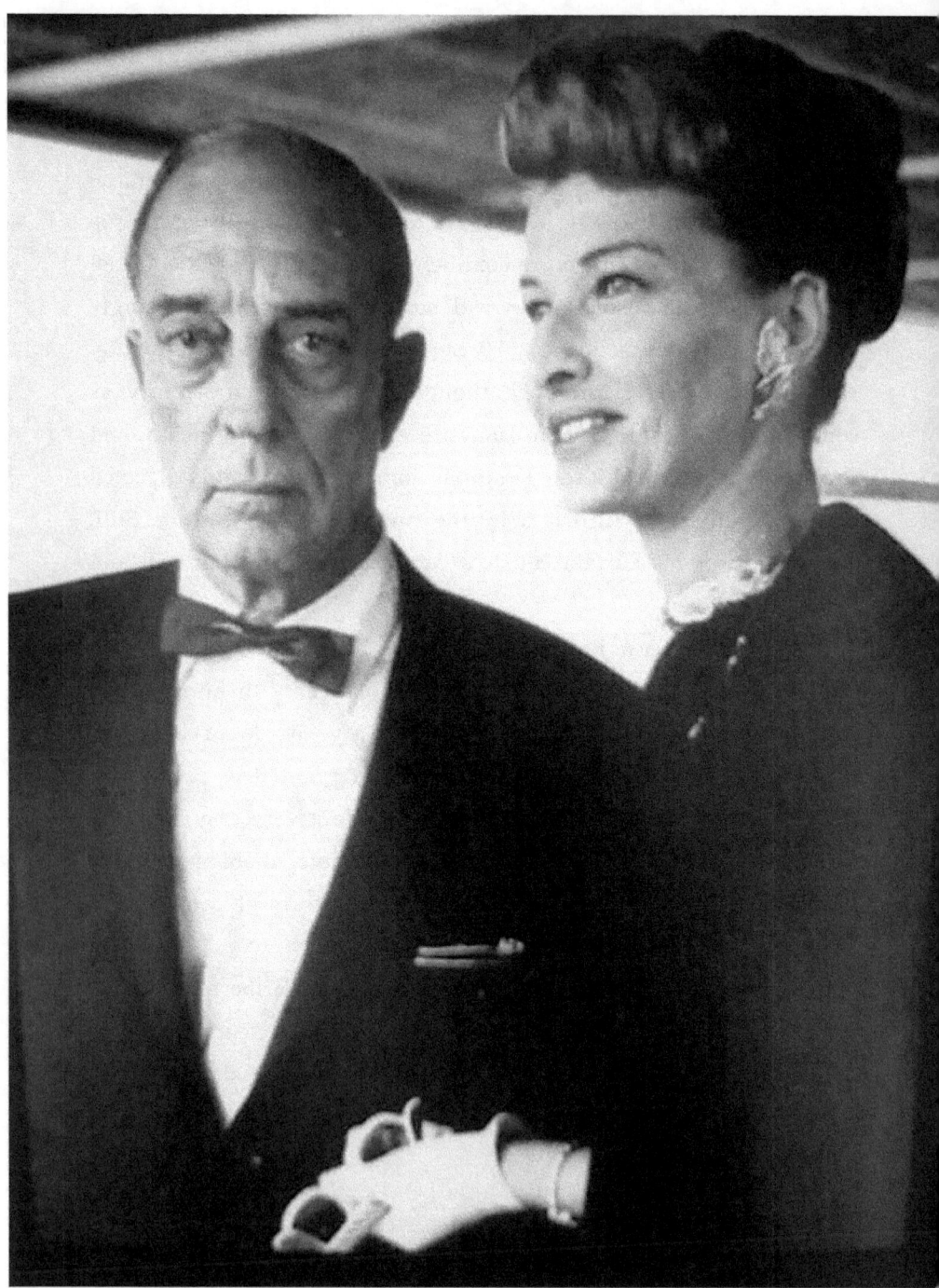

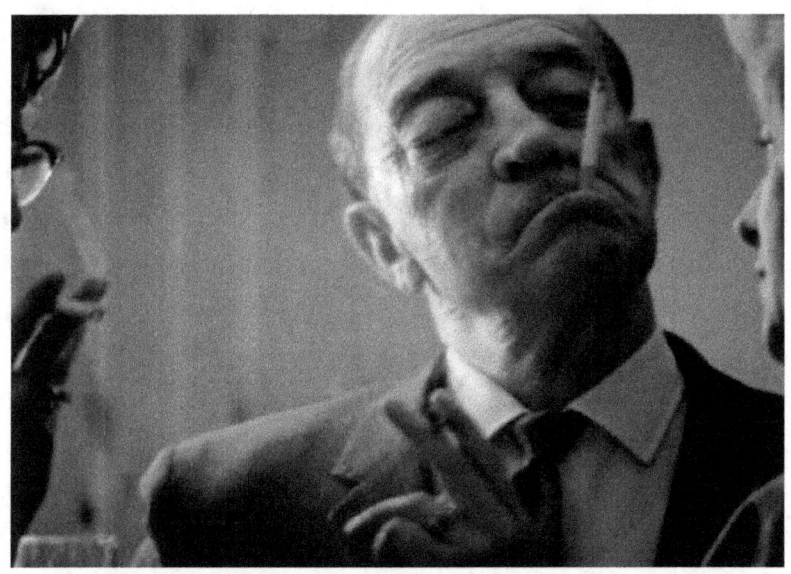

THE DEATH AND IMMORTALITY
OF BUSTER KEATON

"Keaton was very down on himself... he didn't have any ego.
He always felt that his films could have been better,
and that he was not successful...."
- Raymond Rohauer

"I have so many projects coming up, I haven't time to think about kicking the bucket," Buster said shortly before his death, unaware of what was around the corner. "People are always telling me I'm immortal, and I just might prove them right!" He was kind of right; he would become immortal, although not physically, but in his work.

155

Buster sounded in good spirits, and that was because he had reason to be. In 1957, they made a film about him, The Buster Keaton Story, a rather inaccurate biopic. Not only did it enhance Buster's reputation, the grosses from it helped pay for Buster a nice modest home, a haven he called The Ranch. He enjoyed a wonderful life there, having friends over, being the king of his castle and playing with his train set in the garage. In fact, the renowned train enthusiast had a locomotive that went all around the whole house, even carrying food in its carriages at meal times. "He had tracks that made giant circles around the picnic table. One would carry three hard boiled eggs and the other would carry olives. He'd stop it so everyone could take what they wanted. You'd open the fridge and there'd be freight trains full of food waiting to go out," recalled Eleanor, laughing at the quirky memory years later. Buster was a loveable eccentric playing with his toys, living for the day and whatever it had to offer.

The fact is, Buster did good work in this era, though few would take the time to highlight it. A few Buster fans recognise the joy of this period, in particular the army of Keaton devotees with blogs dedicated to him. On Nitrate Glow, the charms of the final era were not lost on the writer, who wrote "There are many who view the last thirty-something years of Buster Keaton's life as a tragedy worthy of the absurdists, ignoring his own statements about considering himself fabulously lucky. Many Keatonphiles take him at his word nowadays, though it is hard not to be disappointed that after 1928, he was never again behind or in front of the camera on projects like The General or Steamboat Bill Jr. Still, that does not mean his later career is worthless; in fact, there are a lot of moments that are quite fun and rewarding."

While I see this last period as much more than simply fun and rewarding, it is nice to see like-minded admirers of Keaton's last chapter. For me, it's the full circle, Keaton rounding off what he had started and was interrupted from doing by the system.

The strangest thing about the death of Buster Keaton is that he was definitely dying for a month before his eventual passing, though

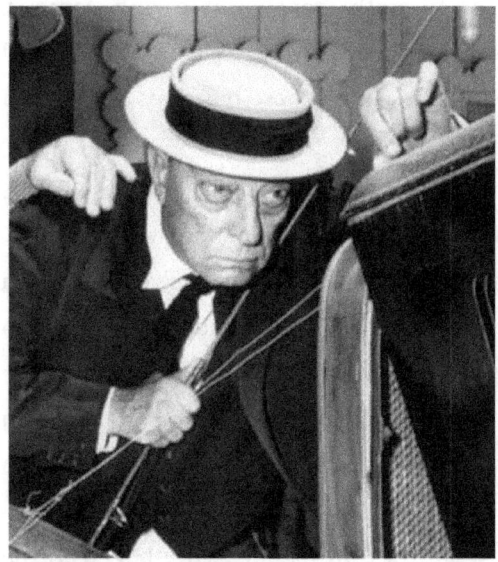

he really didn't know this was the fact. Diagnosed with cancer in January of 1966, nobody told Buster it was terminal. In fact, Keaton did not even know he had cancer at all, figuring he was getting over a spell of Bronchitis. Nevertheless, his body was riddled with it, largely due to a lifetime of smoking. But Keaton kept on trucking, oblivious to the fact that he was in his final days. The cancer was inoperable - all they had to do now was wait.

Keaton ended up in hospital at the very end, but in typical Buster fashion, he was restless and paced his room continuously. He wanted to go home, pure and simple. His wife also said that Buster was in an OK way, even playing cards with visitors, right up until the eve of his death on the 1st of February 1966.

When you look at the facts laid out, Keaton enjoyed an amazingly fruitful last year. He was at his most employed for years. Keaton, went out very much in demand and at the top of his game. Had he known he was dying however, things could have been very different.

After he died, Keaton's reputation as a cinematic giant only heightened, until he became recognised as one of the big three - up there with Chaplin, and Harold Lloyd, who enjoyed a similar renaissance after his death due to re-runs of his films. Though Chaplin remained the more instantly recognisable and famous, Keaton became just as influential, especially to filmmakers, and though nowhere near as iconic as Chaplin, those bug eyes became an immovable part of film history.

Mel Brooks: "There are many words said about Buster Keaton. They usually use the word 'genius.' I don't think he was a genius. Einstein was a genius; Buster Keaton was astonishing. I've never seen any human being able to perform as brilliantly and gracefully with such unusually gifted timing. There was only one Keaton."

Woody Allen: "I know of only six genuine comic geniuses in movie history; Charlie Chaplin, Buster Keaton, Groucho Marx, Harpo Marx, Peter Sellers and WC Fields."

The true turn around in Keaton's film legacy really began in the mid 1950s, when Keaton met film collector and distributor/business man Raymond Rohauer, who was a massive Keaton fan and wanted to strike up business with him. In 1954, they began a proper partnership that would ensure Keaton's movies got shown in cinemas all over the world. Raymond met Buster at a screening of The General in LA. "I was in the projection room," Raymond recalled. "I got a ring that Buster Keaton was in the lobby. I go down and there he is with Eleanor. The next day I met with him at his home. I didn't realize we were going to join forces. But I realized he had this I-don't-care attitude about his stuff. He said, 'It's valueless. I don't own the rights.'"

Buster did have some prints of various classic movies (Sherlock Jr. for example, and Three Ages) and James Mason, who was then living in the home Keaton had owned in his heyday, found various reels in the basement, and handed them on to Buster. Had he not obtained these vital prints, and met Raymond for that matter, who knows if Keaton's legacy would be what it is today. There is only one Keaton film not in existence (a short with Arbuckle no less, A Country Hero), and over time long lost movies have surfaced. Though Rohauer's character and practices have come under a spell of criticism, there is no doubt that Buster trusted him, and he did only good for his legacy.

Keaton and his new business partner toured the world screening his old films. Keaton could not have predicted the reactions to what he saw as forgotten, inconsequential old relics. Standing outside one cinema, he asked Rohauer what everyone was laughing about inside. "It's your movie Buster," chuckled Rohauer, "he couldn't believe it. He didn't say anything, he just listened."

In 1965, he was honoured at the Venice Film Festival. The recognition he received there meant the world to him, not to mention the roaring standing ovation. His collaboration with Beckett was shown, and earned a highly regarded award. (Interesting note, at the New York Film Festival, it was shown as part of a Buster retrospective and was met with harsh boos.) It went to show that filmgoers did appreciate his new films, if they got the chance to see them that is.

As time went on, Buster's films began to look better and better. Rather than dating, they revealed new details and charm, the stunts seemed more unbelievable and daring (especially in the modern era of health and safety) and the things he managed to achieve as a director seemed to be more miraculous.

In his book The Birth of Cinema, published in 1974 interestingly, nearly a decade after Keaton's death though still in Chaplin's life time, DJ Wenden writes, "His (Keaton's) reputation has soared while that of Chaplin has declined. Keaton's philosophy of bewildered contempt for his innumerable enemies and his acceptance of misfortune command more favour than the busyness of Chaplin. Charlie worked hard for his laughs and now that his tricks are well known the laughs are harder to come by. But although Keaton is now more highly regarded there is no doubt that fifty years ago Chaplin was more universally popular and is more significant in the history of cinema."

And I believe Winden's words summarise it pretty well. To the average person, even one with only a passing knowledge of silent comedy, Chaplin is "it", an icon whose image has lasted a century now, and promises to last many more, if not for eternity. For those in the know, the silent buffs so to speak, Keaton is King, but it is probably much harder for a newcomer to chance upon Keaton's work than it is Chaplin's. That said, his cult is growing, and a search online reveals thousands of Buster Keaton devotees, many of whom (perhaps most of, in fact) were born after the legend died.

So what of Keaton's later years? Where do the films *really* stand in that rich filmography, that huge career of scaling heights and dismal lows. Well, quite simply, somewhere in the middle. I have spent a whole book dissecting and celebrating work that few seem to care much for, so perhaps my views are a minority. While the later credits are all good in their own way, I would be a fool to say that any of the work, save perhaps the knowing brilliance of The Railrodder, really matches the innovation and skill of his classic pictures. Much of it is as effective, but in different ways. There is a sweetness to it, a warmth, a sadness even. Buster's final work induces mixed feelings.

But it is a respectable closing chapter, a decade and half where he not only became known to the TV crowd, but to a whole new generation of film goers and filmmakers. Buster Keaton saw his reputation rise in his own lifetime, but even he would not believe how his legacy has panned out. Fans born after his life time take the idea of Keaton being a legend and innovator for granted (me included, as someone born in the 1980s well aware that Keaton was one of cinema's early auteurs and true pioneers), and today it seems hard to believe there was a time when the studio had him on a hundred dollars a week providing gags for movies, most of which were never even used. The idea of Keaton giving advice behind the scenes clashes hard with his legendary cinematic creations.

He may have once been forgotten, but thanks to the digital age, his films will never perish, and they will last forever. As long as people want to laugh and enjoy well crafted cinema, Buster Keaton will be a name that keeps popping up. If his influence will last or increase is anyone's guess, but for now at least Keaton is an immortal, long dead but living on forever, on screens all over the world.

"It was a great life," Buster said in his old age, "it sure was..."

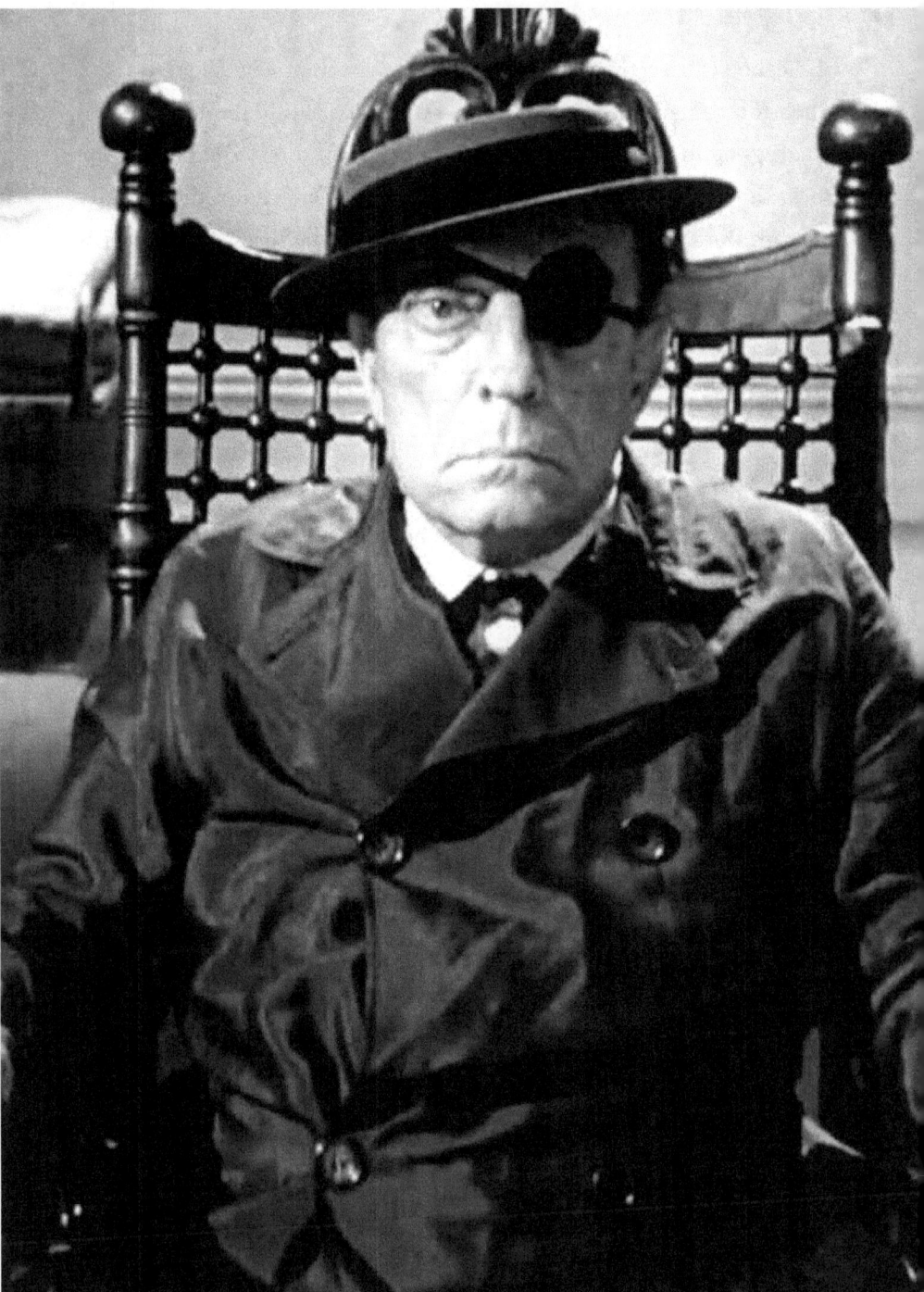

Reference and Acknowledgements

Thanks to Gerald Potterton for his recollections of Buster.

The following sources were helpful too;

Books

Buster Keaton by Tom Dardis

Buster Keaton Interviews

The Fall of Buster Keaton, by James Neibaur

My Wonderful World of Slapstick, by Buster Keaton

Buster Keaton: Cut to the Chase, by Marion Meade

The Birth of Cinema, by DJ Wenden

Documentaries

Buster Keaton: The Genius Crushed By Hollywood

Buster Keaton: A Hard Act to Follow

The Real Buster Keaton

Paul Merton's Silent Clowns: Buster Keaton

Publications and sites;

AV Club

Silentology

Variety

Life Magazine

Photoplay

Time Out

ABOUT CHRIS WADE

Chris Wade is a UK based writer and musician. As well as running the acclaimed music project Dodson and Fogg, he has written books on Dennis Hopper, Madonna, Bob Dylan and many more. He has also released audiobooks of his comedic fiction, narrated by such actors as Rik Mayall. His other projects include Rainsmoke, a musical outfit with actor Nigel Planer, and Hound Dawg Magazine. His first film, The Apple Picker, featured Toyah Willcox, and was released in 2017.

More info at his website: wisdomtwinsbooks.weebly.com